THE MINDFUL MAKER

THE MINDFUL MAKER

35 creative fabric projects to focus the mind and soothe the soul

clare youngs

CICO BOOKS
LONDON NEW YORK

Published in 2019 by CICO Books
An imprint of Ryland Peters & Small Ltd
20–21 Jockey's Fields   341 E 116th St
London WC1R 4BW   New York, NY 10029

www.rylandpeters.com

10 9 8 7 6 5 4 3 2 1

Text © Clare Youngs 2019
Design, illustration, and photography
© CICO Books 2019

A CIP catalog record for this book is available from the
Library of Congress and the British Library.

ISBN: 978 1 78249 788 2

Printed in China

Editor: Clare Sayer
Designer: Elizabeth Healey
Photographer: Joanna Henderson
Stylist: Clare Youngs
Illustrator: Ian Youngs
Techniques illustrations: Stephen Dew (pages 10–11)

In-house editor: Anna Galkina
Art director: Sally Powell
Production manager: Gordana Simakovic
Publishing manager: Penny Craig
Publisher: Cindy Richards

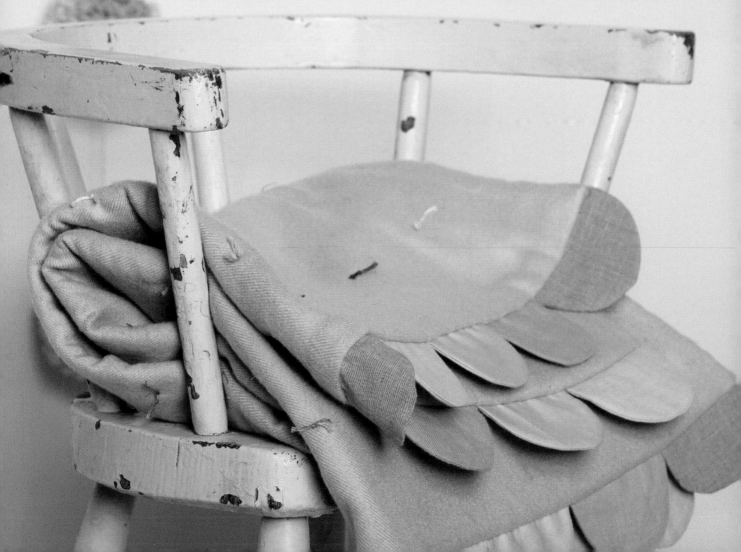

CONTENTS

Introduction 6

Techniques 8

CHAPTER 1

MINDFUL HOME 12

Felt planters 14

Pompom throw 16

Punch-needled footstool 18

Big and bold leaf pillow 20

Indigo woven mat 23

Latch hook pillow 26

Zigzag bowls 29

Jute-covered lamp 32

Color block quilt 35

Sashiko stitched coasters 38

CHAPTER 2

THOUGHTFUL GIFTS 40

Embroidered shirt 42

Little acorn covered buttons 44

Tasseled tree decorations 46

Splatter tote bag 48

Doodle notebooks 51

Boro stitched jeans 54

Knot stitched linen bag 57

Soft leather pouches 60

Wave stitched craft bag 62

Rainbow-handled string bag 65

Floral needlepoint cards 68

CHAPTER 3

TACTILE GIFTS FOR KIDS 70

Leaping horse softie 72

Scallop edged baby quilt 75

Nordic Christmas stockings 78

Mini menagerie pin badges 82

Raindrop cloud mobile 84

Fluffy koala bag 87

Squeezy kitty 90

CHAPTER 4

CREATIVE WALL ART 94

Abstract framed needlepoint 96

Copper hoop macramé 98

Coral-inspired embroidery hoops 101

Leaping tiger wall art 104

Art deco wall hanging 107

Delicate floral wall hanging 110

Textured weave 112

Templates 116

Suppliers 127

Index 128

Acknowledgments 128

INTRODUCTION

Mindfulness has become a bit of a buzzword in recent years. There has been much talk about **slowing down**, **enjoying the moment**, and leading a less stressful life. Let's face it: life can be pretty hectic. The day-to-day whirlwind of work, families, household chores, and keeping up a social life while rushing around needing to do things and be places can take a toll on our mental and **physical wellbeing**. At the same time, we are being bombarded by constant imagery, messages, and content from our digital devices—we need time out. Taking up a craft can be one way of **relieving** that **stress** and **tension**.

As a child I didn't have computer games or mobile phones and even the television didn't have the limitless choice of channels we have today. So I made things! I learned to sew, knit, and crochet, starting out with doll's clothes and then, in my teenage years, making things I wanted to buy, but couldn't afford. Later, when I had my first home, I made curtains, pillows, and chair covers. What I remember, besides being quite pleased that I had saved a lot of money by doing it myself, was that feeling of achievement and happiness in the actual physical making. Later still, when raising four children and squeezing work in between, I sometimes needed to **escape and unwind**; when I could, being creative and making something was the way I was able to achieve this and gain a sense of **calm**. When you are making something, the mind is focused, and often the action you are doing is repetitive, which is soothing—almost meditative—pushing out any negative thoughts you may have. It is all about getting the **"flow,"** which is the perfect state between **concentration** and **action**. When you are there in the zone, the everyday world drops away and any stress and worries along with it.

Of course it's not always possible to take yourself off for hours, to immerse yourself in a long project, so that is when small pieces of hand sewing come into their own. You can keep them handy nearby for when you have some moments and the need to unwind, or you could even pop them into your bag for a bit of mindfulness on-the-go. I am not really happy on airplanes and these small pieces of sewing have kept me **calm** and **relaxed** in what to me would be a stressful experience.

Many people all over the world are finding how beneficial it is to learn a craft and there are workshops and groups to join everywhere. If there isn't one near you, maybe you could start one? They are a great way for some social interaction, especially if you are a shy type and lacking in confidence.

I have put together 35 projects using fabrics and textiles. There are hand-stitched projects, alongside machine sewing, punch needling, weaving, needlepoint, and more. Among the projects you will find unique and beautiful wall hangings and pillows, cute things for kids, greetings cards, and stylish things for your home. Many of the projects would make wonderful gifts for friends and family, and you will have the satisfaction and pleasure of knowing that they have been **lovingly handcrafted** and will be treasured. Some of the crafts may be new to you but I hope you will give those a go. I'd like to think you will gain as much happiness from creating as I do and become **super-chilled in the process!**

TECHNIQUES

TRANSFERRING PATTERNS AND MOTIFS

Most of the projects in this book use some kind of template, to be used either as a cutting guide, for example when cutting pieces for the Fluffy Koala Bag (see page 87), or as a stitch guide, as in the Little Acorn Covered Buttons (see page 44). If a template needs to be enlarged it will clearly say by what percentage; otherwise you can assume that the templates can be used at actual size.

In some of the projects, you will have to transfer the embroidery pattern or motif onto the fabric. I use three different methods. The first—and the easiest—is tracing. If the fabric is sheer enough, lay it over the pattern and trace it, using a dressmaker's fade-away marker pen. Alternatively, tape the pattern to a window with the fabric on top, and draw over the lines of the pattern. The second method is for thick or dark fabrics. Lay dressmaker's carbon paper on the fabric, carbon side down. Lay the embroidery pattern on top and trace over the motif with a ballpoint pen. You can buy carbon paper in different colors suitable for different fabrics. The final method is for the few fabrics that have a fluffy pile and are difficult to draw on. Trace the motif onto a piece of white tissue paper and pin it onto the fabric. Using cotton sewing thread and a closely spaced running stitch, baste (tack) through the tissue paper and fabric along the pattern lines. Remove the tissue paper, complete the embroidery, and then remove the basting (tacking) stitches.

PUNCH NEEDLING

Punch needling is a technique of making loops in a fabric; by making these loops closer together you form an area of color. You work from the back, which is seen as a smooth stitch, while the front is the looped section. I do like both textures and sometimes plan the back to be the front! To make these loops you use a tool called a punch needle, which is easily found in most craft shops. The needles have a hollow shaft and a depth gauge—the eye of the needle is positioned at the end of this sharp metal section. The needles come in different sizes; the different sizes make different sized loops. The projects in this book are all made with chunky yarn so I used a size 10 needle that makes ¼ inch (5 mm) loops.

The best fabric to use is monk's cloth but it can be quite difficult to get hold of in the UK. You can use a thick loose-weave linen, or something similar, as an alternative.

For small punch needle projects that use a fine needle, you can use an embroidery hoop to hold your fabric. It is best to use one that has a ridge that locks the two hoops together. This is important as the action of punching can loosen the fabric, and to be able to stitch, the fabric must be very taut.

For the projects in this book you will need a frame. You can buy these from craft suppliers but I made mine from an old picture frame and some carpet tack strip. Cut lengths of carpet tack strip into four sections that fit the four sides of your frame. Nail these into the frame all the way around, making sure that the sharp tacks are facing out.

There are instructions on how to place the fabric on the frame and how to protect yourself from the sharp tacks in the Punch-needled Footstool project on page 18 so do refer closely to these pages before you start punch needling. The most important thing to remember is that the fabric should be very taut across the frame.

Some tips on getting a good stitch

Thread the yarn through the shaft and out through the eye in the metal depth gauge.

1 Hold the punch needle as you would a pen, making sure the yarn falls loosely over the back of your hand. Place the sharp tip, where you want to start. You will see there is a slanted cut section in the tip—this needs to be facing the direction you are stitching at all times. Push the needle down into the fabric, right down the length of the metal depth gauge so the beginning of the handle section touches the fabric. If you don't do the whole length then you will pull out the loop and it will come undone.

2 Then pull the needle back out toward you—but only just. The tip of the needle should remain on the surface of the fabric; move it along to make the next stitch. There isn't an exact measurement of where to place the next stitch; you want it to be close enough to form a solid block of color but slightly away so that there is enough fabric to hold the stitch. With some practice you will be able to judge this by eye and move quickly. I like to outline an area with a row of stitches and then punch around in rows to finish off. If you make a mistake, it is easy to pull out the loops and redo them.

3 When you have completed a section, slowly pull the needle up while being careful not to pull the last hoop out. Snip the yarn, leaving an end about ¾ in. (2 cm) long. Use a small pair of scissors with the blades closed to push this gently through to the other side. This can then be snipped off to the same length as the loops and won't be visible in the finished project.

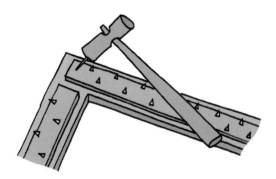

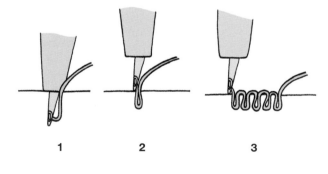

1 2 3

STRAIGHT STITCH

Straight stitches can be used on their own or arranged to form other embroidery stitches.

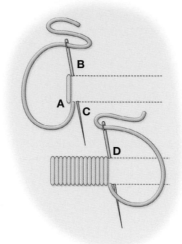

SATIN STITCH

This is a "filler" stitch that is useful for motifs such as flower petals and leaves. Work from left to right. Draw the shape on the fabric, then work straight stitches across it, coming up at A and down at B, then up at C and down at D, and so on. Place the stitches next to each other, so that no fabric can be seen between them. You can also work a row of backstitch around the edge to define the outline more clearly.

DETACHED CHAIN STITCH

Bring the needle up through the fabric and reinsert it at the same point. Bring it back up a short distance away, looping the thread around the needle tip. Pull the thread through and then fasten the stitch by taking a small vertical stitch across the bottom of the loop

DAISY STITCH

Work a group of six to eight detached chain stitches in a circle to form a flower shape.

BLANKET STITCH

Working from left to right, bring the needle through at the edge of the fabric. Push the needle back through the fabric a stitch width and length to the right and loop the thread under the needle. Pull the needle and thread to make the first stitch. Make another stitch to the right in the same way and continue along the fabric.

When you get to a corner, push the needle back through the bottom of the last stitch and then take the needle up to the corner point, looping the thread under the needle as before.

BACKSTITCH

Make a single straight stitch, bringing the needle out again one stitch length ahead. Make the next stitch back into the end of the first stitch to make one backstitch. To continue, bring the needle out again a stitch length in front of the previous stitch each time and work back into the end of the previous stitch.

WHIPPED BACKSTITCH

Work a line of backstitches. Using a blunt needle, slide the needle under the thread of the first backstitch from top to bottom and pull the thread through. Repeat in each alternate stitch in the row.

FRENCH KNOT

Bring the needle up from the back of the fabric to the front. Wrap the thread two or three times around the tip of the needle, then reinsert the needle at the point where it first emerged, holding the wrapped threads with the thumbnail of your non-stitching hand, and pull the needle all the way through. The wraps will form a knot on the surface of the fabric.

BULLION KNOT

This is similar to a French knot, but creates a longer coil of thread rather than a single knot. Bring the needle up at A and take it down at B, leaving a loose loop of thread—the distance from A to B being the length of knot that you require.

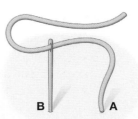

Bring the needle back up at A and wrap the thread around the needle three to five times for a shorter knot, or five to eight times for a longer knot. Hold the wrapped thread in place with your left hand and pull the needle all the way through.

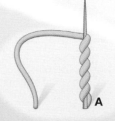

Insert the needle at B and pull through, easing the coiled stitches neatly into position.

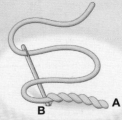

MINDFUL HOME

FELT PLANTERS

POMPOM THROW

PUNCH-NEEDLED FOOTSTOOL

BIG AND BOLD LEAF PILLOW

INDIGO WOVEN MAT

LATCH HOOK PILLOW

ZIGZAG BOWLS

JUTE-COVERED LAMP

COLOR BLOCK QUILT

SASHIKO STITCHED COASTERS

FELT PLANTERS

Bringing **NATURE** into our homes is **GOOD FOR** our **WELLBEING**. As well as having a **CALMING** effect, looking after houseplants helps us to **LOOK OUTWARD** so that we are not stuck in over-thinking. I used an offcut of lovely thick felt for this slipcover and added a **SATISFYING** simple stitched design. The pale leather thongs used to hang the planter and pale gray of the felt contrasts nicely with the green foliage, for a fresh and contemporary look to **BRIGHTEN UP** the darker and gloomier winter months.

YOU WILL NEED (FOR 2 PLANTERS)

2 pieces of thick ⅛ in. (4 mm) felt, approximately 4 x 13 in. (10.5 x 33 cm)

2 plastic pots, 4 in. (10 cm) in diameter

Pencil

Ruler

Six-stranded embroidery floss (thread) in a color that contrasts with the felt

Needle

Hole punch

Matching sewing thread

Bradawl

Scissors

6 lengths of leather thong, approximately 30 in. (80 cm) in length

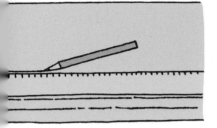

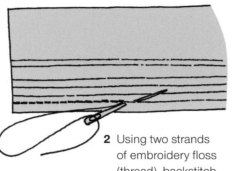

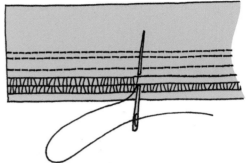

1 Check that your felt strip fits around your plant pot—the ends should overlap by ½ in. (1 cm). Using the pencil and ruler, draw a line across the length of the felt, ½ in. (1 cm) up from the bottom edge. Draw three more lines at ½ in. (1 cm) intervals. Draw the next line with a ¾ in. (1.5 cm) gap and the final line with a ¼ in. (5 mm) gap.

2 Using two strands of embroidery floss (thread), backstitch along the lines, covering the pencil lines.

3 Make vertical stitches between the horizontal lines, making sure that the stitches touch the horizontal lines with no gap. The stitches can slope either way and can vary in the way they are spaced apart. Continue to stitch between all the lines.

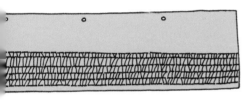

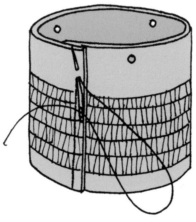

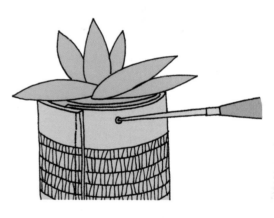

4 Starting from the top right side of the felt, measure 4 in. (10 cm) along and mark with a pencil, ¾ in. (1.5 cm) down from the top edge. Make two more marks with 4 in. (10 cm) gaps between. (If your planter is a slightly different size, you may need to adjust these measurements; the idea is to make the holes evenly spaced when the felt is wrapped around the pot.)

5 Use a hole punch to punch holes at these points—my hole punch is adjustable so I made my holes ⅛ in. (4 mm) across but a wider hole will work as well. Bring the two ends of the strip of felt together, overlapping the ends to form a tube. Pin and stitch with small backstitches, matching the thread color to the felt color.

6 Place the plant in its pot inside the tube. Use a pen to mark through the holes in felt onto the plastic pot and then push through the holes with something sharp like a bradawl. You may also be able to punch the holes in the plastic pot with your hole punch.

7 Thread the leather thongs through the holes in the felt and the pot and secure each one with a knot. Tie the three thongs together at the top. Your plant is now ready to hang.

POMPOM THROW

This is a wonderfully **TACTILE** project—aside from enjoying the feel of the fluffy pompoms, you can put the blanket over you as you stitch, and appreciate the **LUXURIOUS FEEL** of the woolen fabric. Although you can use a pompom maker, it's **THERAPEUTIC** to make the pompoms in the traditional way. The repetitive nature of winding the wool is **CALMING** and it's **SATISFYING** to see the 14 pompoms lined up in a row. I matched the yarn to the floss (thread), but you can use contrasting colors.

YOU WILL NEED

Length of woolen fabric—mine measured 43 x 55 in. (110 x 140 cm)

Pins

Six-stranded embroidery floss (thread)

Embroidery needle

Cardboard (an old cereal box is a good thickness)

Scissors

Woolen yarn

Pompom maker (optional)

1 Fold over and pin a double ½ in. (1 cm) hem along all four sides of the fabric.

2 Following the instructions on page 10 and using six strands of embroidery floss (thread), blanket stitch around all four sides of the throw.

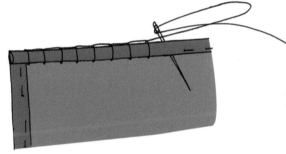

3 Cut out two cardboard circles measuring 2¼ in. (6 cm) in diameter, and cut out the center of the circle, as shown in the illustration on the left. Place them together, matching up the section that is cut out. Start winding the wool round and round the cardboard. Continue until you have a nice fat amount of wound wool. Cut the yarn and hold in place with your thumb while you use scissors to cut around the edge of the pompom, slipping your scissors between the two cardboard circles. Take a length of yarn and tie it tightly around the center of the pompom, between the cardboard circles, then gently remove the cardboard and fluff up the pompom. Repeat to make 14 pompoms in total. (Alternatively use a pompom maker, if you have one.)

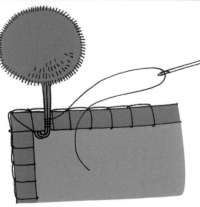

4 Cut the ties on the pompoms down to 2 in. (5 cm). Space seven of the pompoms evenly along two opposite sides of the reverse of the throw. Tuck the ends of the ties into the hem, in between the blanket stitches, and secure with a few stitches.

PUNCH-NEEDLED FOOTSTOOL

TUNE IN to the colors and shapes of this creative project. Enjoy the repetitive and **CALMING** nature of working the needle and the **SATISFACTION** of seeing the color blocks building up. Cutting up colored paper is a good way to try out designs and a **SOOTHING** activity in itself. Use the template on page 125 and adjust the measurements to fit (include the sides of the stool)—the simple shapes can be adapted to any size..

YOU WILL NEED

Template on page 125

Paper, pencil, and pen

Wooden frame (see page 9)

Monk's cloth or a loose weave linen fabric-enough to cover the top and sides of your footstool with an extra 2 in. (5 cm) all round to attach the fabric to the underside of the stool

Thick felt cut into 1½ in. (4 cm) strips

Needle and basting (tacking) thread

No. 10 punch needle

Chunky yarn in assorted colors

Small pointed scissors

Footstool

Staple gun

1 Draw up your design onto the cloth; you can design your own or use the template on page 125. If you have drawn your design onto paper, use some sticky tape to secure it in place on a window. Place the monk's cloth over the template, making sure that there is an even border around the edge. Secure the cloth with some sticky tape. Trace over the lines with a pen (the pen lines will all be covered up by the design).

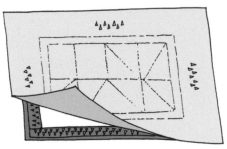

2 To attach the cloth to the frame, lay the fabric down over the frame, making sure that the design is centered and there is an even amount of fabric extending on all sides. The fabric has to be very taut as you will not be able to punch into loose fabric. I start by hooking over a section from the middle of each side to get a good tension, all the while making sure that the design is straight and centered. Then hook the rest of the fabric. You can carry on lifting and stretching the fabric all around until it is really tight. Be careful, as the nails in the frame will be very sharp.

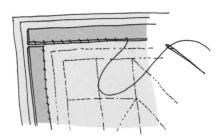

3 Cut some thick felt to the lengths of the sides of the frame. Double or triple it over if it is not thick. Baste (tack) these strips to the sides of the frame to cover the nails around the edges of the design. You need to do this to protect your arms as you work; it doesn't take long and it is important!

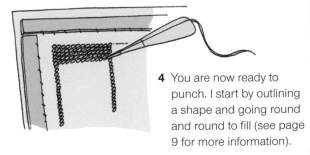

4 You are now ready to punch. I start by outlining a shape and going round and round to fill (see page 9 for more information).

5 When you have completed your design and finished off all the loose ends, remove the tacked-on felt and unhook the cloth from the nails and remove it from the frame. The fabric will have stretch holes, where the nails were, but these disappear with a bit of rubbing.

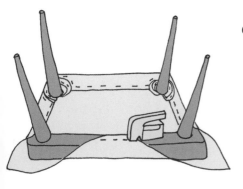

6 Lay the piece over the footstool. Trim off any extra fabric if you need to—there should be enough fabric at the edge to tuck beneath and staple to the underside of the stool. Turn the footstool over and, using the staple gun, start attaching the fabric. It is best to staple the center of each side first to get a good tension. Tuck the fabric in neatly around the legs and staple down.

7 At the corners, fold the fabric at right angles, pull the cloth tightly underneath the stool, and use the staple gun to secure.

NOTES In the Techniques section on page 9 you will find more detailed instructions on how to use your punch needle and tips for successful needling. Practice before you get going on a larger project. The great thing about this craft is that it is very easy to undo parts to redo them!

BIG AND BOLD LEAF PILLOW

A real statement piece—there's something very **MESMERIZING** about this striking design, which is made using a punch needle. One side is made up of loops and this is generally used for the front; the other side has a more compact stitch. You can use either here—I like both but I thought the more compact stitch makes the design on this project stand out sharply.

1 Enlarge the template on page 116 to the right size. If you are using printer paper, you will need to enlarge the design in sections and stick them together with some sticky tape.

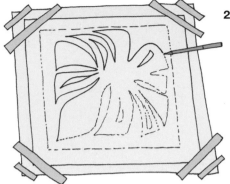

2 To transfer the design onto the fabric, use some sticky tape to attach the paper template to a window. Place the cloth over the top and use the tape to secure it in place. Go over the lines. You can use a pen as the lines will all be covered up by the design.

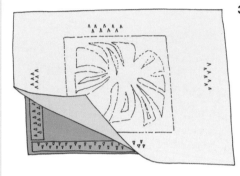

3 To attach the cloth to the frame, lay the fabric over the frame, making sure that the design is centered and there is an even amount of fabric extending on all sides. The fabric has to be very taut as you will not be able to punch into loose fabric. I start by hooking over a section from the middle of each side to get a good tension, all the while making sure that the design is straight and centered. Then hook the rest of the fabric—you can carry on lifting and stretching the fabric, all around, until it is really tight. Be careful, as the nails in the frame are very sharp.

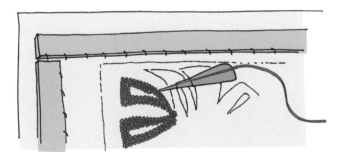

4 Cut some thick felt to the lengths of the sides of the frame. Double or triple it over if it is not thick enough. Baste (tack) these strips to the sides of the frame to cover the nails. You need to do this to protect your arms; it doesn't take long and it is important!

5 Start punching the design. Remember that with punch-needling, the side you normally work on becomes the back (with the looped side on the reverse) but with this project, if you want the flat stitch at the front, you will actually be punching into the front of the pillow, so you have to be extra careful to punch neatly as mistakes show a little bit more with the flat stitches. I did mine in sections. I chose a section of the leaf, punched in the outline, and then went round and round filling in, before moving on to the next section (see Techniques on page 9). That leaves the middle part of the leaf to finish off last.

I then moved on to punch the background. Because I used monk's cloth, which has lines printed on it, I wanted to cover the complete background with stitches. If you have used linen, you may want to leave the fabric as the background.

6 When you have finished the design, remove the tacked-on felt protectors and unhook the cloth. There will be stretched holes made from the nails but these disappear with some rubbing. Trim all around the edge of the design, leaving a ¾ in. (2 cm) border of unpunched cloth.

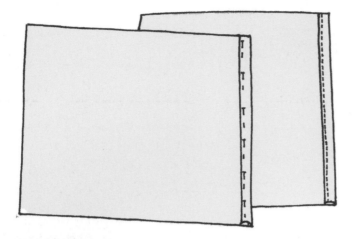

7 Take one of the pieces of backing fabric. Turn over a ½ in. (1 cm) double hem along one edge and pin and stitch in place. Repeat along one edge of the other piece.

8 Place the punched cloth with the loop side facing down on to a flat surface. With right sides together, place the larger backing piece on top, aligning the unhemmed edge and the two side seams. Pin in position—you are aiming to sew as close to edge of the loops as you can.

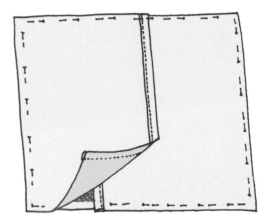

9 With the right side facing down, place the smaller backing piece over the top at the other end of the front piece, so that it overlaps the larger piece. Pin in position, making sure you pin through all three layers, alongside the looped stitches.

10 Use a sewing machine to stitch all around the four sides, pushing back the loops if they are getting in the way, so that you can sew up close to this edge. Trim off any spare fabric down to about ½ in. (1 cm); monk's cloth does fray, so if you have used it, it is a good idea to run a zigzag stitch all around the raw edges.

11 Turn the pillow cover the right way out and insert your pillow pad.

NOTES In the Techniques section on page 9 you will find more detailed instructions on how to use your punch needle and tips for successful needling. Practice before you get going on a larger project. The great thing about this craft is that it is very easy to undo parts to redo them! See page 9 for how to make a frame.

INDIGO WOVEN MAT

I find looking through my vintage craft books a wonderful **MINDFUL** activity in itself. Those produced in the seventies include lots of colorful weavings—a craft that has gained popularity again, with textile artists producing beautiful and **TACTILE** pieces. You need a small wooden loom and some yarn, but you can also create wonderful and unusual pieces using fabric. I noticed the lovely frayed selvage edge on some indigo dyed fabric in my stash recently. I thought it was too good to hide away under a hem, so have designed a mat showcasing those edges, made from longs strips of the cloth. The finished result has a lovely textural quality and there was real **SENSORY PLEASURE** in making it. You could use denim for a more robust finish.

YOU WILL NEED

A wooden loom

Twine (I used natural jute)

Strips of fabric

Scissors

Large blunt darning needle with an eye that will take a strip of fabric

Needle and cotton

Pins

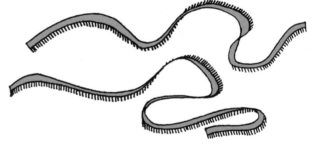

1 Prepare the loom with the warp threads—these are the threads that are held in tension across the loom. Tie one end of the twine around the side of the loom at the top. Slip the twine into the first notch and take it down to the corresponding notch at the bottom. Go into this notch, along to the next one and then up again to the corresponding notch at the top. Repeat along the entire width of the loom. Tie off the twine to the side of the loom, making sure that the tension is tight.

2 Cut some selvage from the fabric in long strips approximately ½ in. (1 cm) wide (don't worry too much about exact measurements). Fray the strips back a few millimeters. You may not have enough selvedge edge to complete the weaving. If this is the case, cut some strips from the main piece of fabric and fray each side of the strip by a few millimeters.

3 Now you can create the weft—the threads that are woven under and over the warp thread. Thread the needle with a strip of fabric. Starting from either side of the loom, weave the fabric strip under the first warp and over the next, leaving a bit of extra fabric at the beginning to finish off later. Carry on across the width of the loom until you reach the end warp thread.

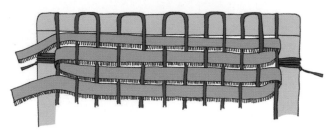

4 Now loop the strip of fabric back over the same warp thread and weave back along the next row. Make sure that the strip is woven in the opposite way to the one above, so if the one above goes over the warp thread, the one on the next row should go under it. Carry on in this way, taking care not to pull too tightly at the edges as this will give the weaving an inward curve. (A loom with a metal bar at each edge avoids this problem.) When you reach the end of each strip of fabric, leave a small length at the edge to finish off later. It is always better to finish a strip at the edge to create a neat finish.

5 When you have filled the loom with weaving, untie the thread you tied to the side of the loom and lift the top and bottom sections to remove the weave from the loom. Thread the side thread onto the needle and finish it off with a few stitches at the back of the weaving, leaving a loop of similar size to the others. Repeat this at the other end.

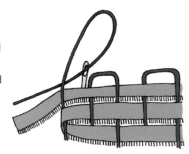

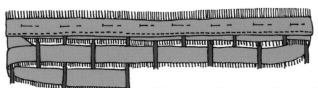

6 Ease the strips of fabric into position, so they sit evenly on the warp thread. Tuck the loose ends of fabric at the edges through to the back of the weaving and finish off with a few stitches.

7 You can either leave the mat like this or finish it off with a frayed edge. Cut two ¾ in. (2 cm) strips from the selvage edge of the fabric that are slightly longer than twice the width of the weaving. Turn under a ¼ in (5 mm) hem. Pin one strip to the top of the weaving, continuing it around the back and overlapping the two ends where they meet. You can use a sewing machine to attach this strip or handstitch it to secure. Repeat at the other edge of the mat.

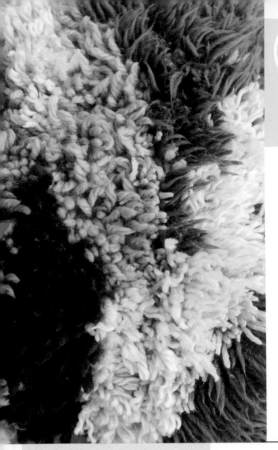

LATCH HOOK PILLOW

Latch hooking is usually used to make rugs but you can make wonderful, fun, and fluffy pillows using the same method, just on a smaller scale. For me this is the **ULTIMATE** in **MINDFUL CRAFT**; it keeps your mind **ALERT** but not overly so, and you can let the **RHYTHM** of the **REPEAT** actions become a very **SOOTHING** occupation. You do not need a lot of equipment—just a simple latch hook tool, a length of latch hook canvas, and some balls of wool. I love the way you can use different colors and different weights of wool to create something beautifully textural and unique.

YOU WILL NEED

Piece of thick card 5½ in. (14 cm) wide

Woolen yarn

Scissors

Latch hook tool

Latch hook canvas, 17½ in. (44 cm) square

Template on page 123

Two pieces of backing fabric: 14½ x 10½ in. (37 x 27 cm) and 14½ x 8 in. (37 x 20 cm)

Pins

Needle and cotton sewing thread

18 in. (45 cm) pillow pad (this is bigger than the pillow cover but will make a nice plump pillow)

NOTE
If you are new to latch hooking, you may find it a good idea to practice using the latch hook and a scrap piece of fabric before you begin the project. Steps 1–5 explain how to hook.

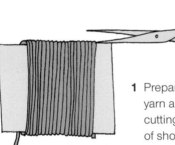

1 Prepare some wool by winding your yarn around the piece of card and cutting top and bottom to make a pile of short lengths of wool.

2 Hold the latch hook in your right hand, or your left hand, if you are left-handed. Take one of your pre-cut pieces of wool and wrap it around the shaft of the latch hook.

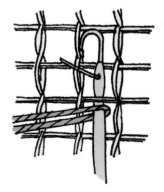

3 Push the end of the latch hook into a hole in the canvas and then out through the hole directly above it. The latch should be open here.

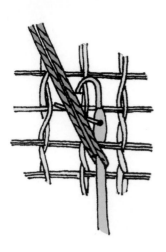

4 Hold the two ends of wool together and position them between the latch and the hook.

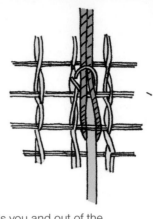

5 Pull the hook towards you and out of the canvas. The latch will close over the wool and you can then pull through to complete the knot. Pull on the two ends evenly to tighten.

6 Now you are ready to start. Draw a 14½ in. (27 cm) square onto your canvas—this is your working square. I have provided a template with suggested areas of color and shape, which you can use for guidance, but really you do not want to be counting squares; it is much better to let the shapes and areas grow organically. It is a lovely way of working that is very freeing.

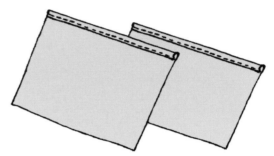

7 When you have finished latch hooking your square, you can now turn it into a pillow cover. Take your two rectangles of backing material and turn over a ½ in. (1 cm) double hem along one long edge on each piece. Pin and stitch in place.

8 Trim the latch canvas back to ¾ in. (2 cm) all around the edge of the worked section and fold in to the edge of the wool section. Fold in a hem on three sides of the rectangle of backing fabric and pin across one end of the pillow. Remember in this case you are pinning the fabric with wrong sides together. Use cotton thread doubled up to hand sew in an overstitch all around three sides.

9 Add the other rectangle at the other end of the pillow in the same way. This rectangle should overlap the first just a little along the sewn hemmed edge. Sew in position. The pillow is ready to fill with the pillow pad.

ZIGZAG BOWLS

This is one of those projects that is so simple to do, but the end result is these stunning little handcrafted bowls. As I was making them, they were already being put to good use for my sewing bits and bobs. I find that you can get into a **RHYTHM** of turning the bowl and going round and round with the zigzag stitch. You have to **CONCENTRATE** a bit, to keep the stitch in the right place, but as you get going, it becomes quite **HYPNOTIC** and you can **LOSE YOURSELF IN THE SPIRALS!**

YOU WILL NEED

Cotton macramé rope, ¼ in. (5 mm) wide

Needle and sewing thread

Sewing machine (use a strong needle if your rope is quite thick)

Small scraps of colored tape, about ¾ in. (1.5 cm) wide

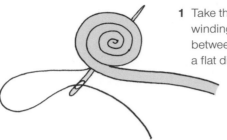

1 Take the end of the cotton rope and start winding it tightly in a spiral, holding it between your thumb and finger, to make a flat disc about 1¼ in. (3 cm) wide.

2 With the needle and thread, sew through the disc from side to side, so that when you take your thumb and finger away, the disc stays together. This will be the base of the bowl.

3 Set your sewing machine to zigzag stitch. Place the needle in the middle and start stitching around in a spiral, trying to get the needle between the coiled rope so that it catches each side, joining the rope together. This is the most difficult bit and you will have to stop the machine every few stitches, lift the foot and turn the disc, to sew the next few stitches.

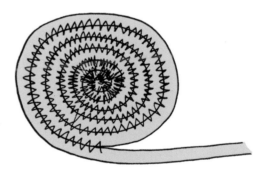

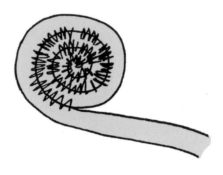

4 Once you get going and the disc gets bigger, it becomes a lot easier to place the needle in the right position and you can carry on going around.

5 As you continue around, the sides will start curving up on their own. Continue until you get to the size you want, then cut off the rope.

6 To make a bigger bowl, start off with a bigger disc, before you place it in the machine. To get the little dots and rectangles of dense stitch, sew some zigzag on the automatic stitch size, then stop the machine, adjust the stitch to a tighter zigzag, continue for a few millimeters and then stop again to put the stitch back to normal.

7 Cut a piece of cotton tape 1½ in. (4 cm) in length. Fold in ½ in. (1 cm) at each end, place over the raw and fraying end of the rope, and pin to the edge of the bowl. Use some small stitches to secure in position.

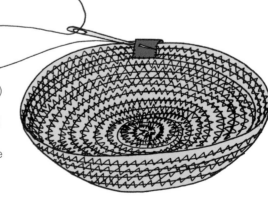

JUTE-COVERED LAMP

YOU WILL NEED

Twine—I used three different colors of 2-ply twine and some waxed linen twine (they usually come in 20 yard/ 20 meter balls)

Wire lampshade frame

Scissors

love using natural fabrics and materials in my crafting. I have a thing about string and twine. The different **TEXTURES** (some smooth, some rough), the way they are wound up, even that **LOVELY** straw basket **SMELL** that the jute twines have! I have used a mix of jute and waxed linen twine here, they are different weights—the linen twine is much thinner—but I like the contrast. The frame I have used is quite an unusual shape. It is more likely that you will find a cone shape, so I have included instructions for both. I have finished mine with a cloth-bound flex that came as a kit with all the light fittings. These are easy to buy now and the flex often comes in a huge variety of colors. Make sure you get an electrician to wire it for you. As you get used to wrapping the twine around the frame, you build up a rhythm that is **REPETITIVE** and **SOOTHING**.

1 Unwind about 6½ yards (6 m) of twine and wind it up into a long thin shape that you can pass through the spokes of the frame. This will make a stripe about 2¾ in. (7 cm) wide on a frame that is 6 in. (15 cm) tall. Tie the end of the twine around the top ring of the frame. Take the twine across to the other side to start.

2 If you are using a frame like mine, take the twine down to the circle of frame at the end of the top straight section. Take the twine under the wire to the back and wind it around the wire, bringing the twine to the front.

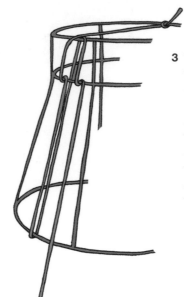

3 Take the twine down to the base of the frame, taking the twine under the rim and back up to the top. Bring the twine over the top and start the sequence again. Continue wrapping around in this way, making sure that you push the strands tightly together at the top. As the lamp frame splays out in a cone shape, the twine will have gaps between them as they come down to the bottom. Even these out, so that the gaps are roughly the same.

4 When you want to change color, cut off the string when you have bought it back up inside and where it is level with the top. Let the twine go so that it falls back down and out at the bottom. Join the next color twine to this end with a knot. Trim the ends back to ¾ in. (2 cm). Then you can take it back up to the top to start winding again. If you do this each time you change color, the ends will all be placed roughly at the same level near the top, and be hidden, because the strands of twine are tight together here.

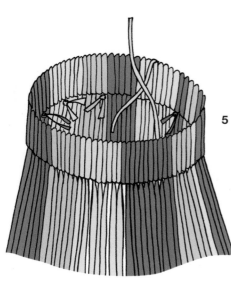

5 When you have covered the whole frame, untie the first strand that was tied across the top and tie it to the last piece of wound string. This time it will be easiest to tie it from the top. Try to position the knot down from the top on the inside, so that it doesn't show. Trim the ends to ¾ in. (2 cm).

6 If you are using a simple cone shaped frame, the instructions are the same but you simply wrap around and around from top to bottom. The knots are best placed in the same position, about 1¼ in. (3 cm) down from the top, on the inside, so they don't show.

COLOR BLOCK QUILT

Although I have been promoting the idea that sewing, especially hand stitching, is good for your **WELLBEING**, I don't think the sewing machine should be banished to the cupboard! Sometimes it is just as relaxing to **FIND SOME TIME TO YOURSELF**, set up your sewing things, and lose yourself in a project. Often, when you are caught up in your busy lifestyle, finding this time can be difficult, but even a short period of time is important and beneficial. When you have completed the project and you are the proud owner of this gorgeous quilt, you will be very pleased with yourself and hopefully super relaxed too!

YOU WILL NEED

Six pieces of fabric
(see step 1)

Scissors

Pins

Sewing machine

One piece of backing fabric
measuring 40¼ x 60 in.
(102 x 152 cm)—you could
repurpose an old duvet cover
or sheet

One piece of thin wadding
the same size as your
backing fabric

1 You can have any combination of squares for your quilt you like, but if you want to follow my layout cut six sections measuring 13 x 20½ in. (32 x 52 cm), five sections measuring 8¾ x 20½ in. (22 x 52 cm), one section measuring 8¾ x 13 in. (22 x 32 cm), and one section measuring 8¾ x 8¾ in. (22 x 22 cm).

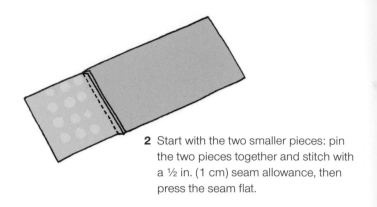

2 Start with the two smaller pieces: pin the two pieces together and stitch with a ½ in. (1 cm) seam allowance, then press the seam flat.

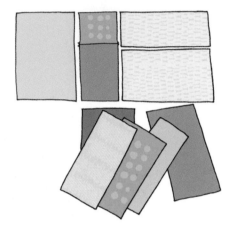

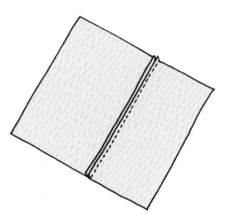

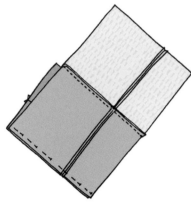

3 You are making up six squares, each containing one large rectangle and one slightly narrower rectangle (the one you have just sewn is a narrower rectangle). Pair the piece made in step 2 with a 13 x 20½ in. (32 x 52 cm) piece. Then pair up the remaining pieces. You can place the squares vertically or horizontally. Move the pieces around until you are happy with the arrangement.

4 Stitch one square at a time—with right sides together, pin the two rectangles together to form a square, then sew together with a ½ in. (1 cm) seam allowance and press flat. Continue until you have made up all the squares.

5 Take three of the squares and with right sides together, pin them together to make a row. Sew the two seams with a ½ in. (1 cm) seam allowance. Repeat this step with the three remaining squares to make another row. Press all the seams flat.

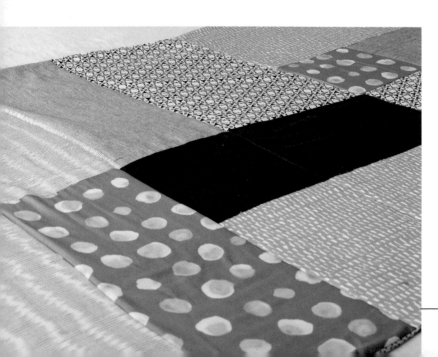

6 Pin the two rows, with right sides together, down the long length. Sew together and press the seams open.

7 Lay the quilted piece out on the floor, right side up. Place the backing fabric on top, with right sides together, and then position the wadding on top, making sure all the edges are aligned. Sew all around the sides with a ½ in. (1 cm) seam allowance, leaving a gap of about 16 in. (40 cm) in one side.

8 Turn the quilt the right way out through the opening, then fold in the raw edges at the opening and sew it closed with small stitches.

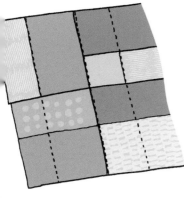

9 Sew a row of stitching across the width of the quilt at different points—don't worry about making the lines of stitching equally spaced apart. I made five lines, using the blocks of fabric as a guide. Press the quilt to finish.

SASHIKO STITCHED COASTERS

Sometimes day-to-day life seems so hectic that we ignore the need to **SLOW DOWN** and take some time out to **REPLENISH** and **SOOTHE** our bodies and minds. Embroidery is the perfect way to **UNWIND**. I like to have a small piece on the go, to pick up and spend a few quiet moments on when days seem impossibly rushed. I have always been fascinated by the art of Japanese sashiko stitching and have wanted to try it. Sashiko was originally used to reinforce and repair clothing in ancient Japan but it is used as a purely decorative stitch too, with many beautiful and intricate patterns formed from the positioning of small straight stitches. This design is called *Hitomezashi Sashiko*, where the pattern emerges from lines of single stitches placed on a grid.

YOU WILL NEED
(FOR 1 COASTER)

Two squares of fabric (I used linen), each 7 x 7 in. (18 x 18 cm)

Ruler

Set square

Air- or heat-erasable pen

Six-stranded embroidery floss (thread)

Needle (look for special sashiko needles, which are longer than the average needle. I used a regular needle, but picked the longest I had)

Stitch guide on page 122

Sewing machine

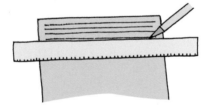

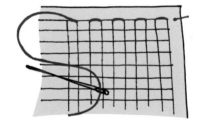

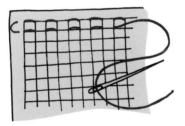

1 Using a setsquare and ruler, draw a grid on one of the squares of fabric, using an air- or heat-erasable pen. Start the grid ½ in. (1 cm) from the top edge and ½ in. (1 cm) in from the side edge. Space the lines ¼ in. (5 mm) apart. If you draw 24 lines across vertically and horizontally you should have a square grid with a border around it.

2 Thread a needle with two strands from a length of embroidery floss (thread) and tie a knot at the end. Starting in the top right corner, take the needle down from the front to the back just in the border. Working from right to left, come up at the top corner of the grid. This is your starting point: make a row of running stitches along the line using the grid as a measure and making one stitch per square. Make a few stitches at a time, gathering the fabric on the needle and then pulling the thread through. This will help you to get an even line of stitches.

3 When you get to the end, bring the needle out in the border, turn the fabric round, and go back along the second row in the same way, matching the stitches. Always leave a loose loop of thread at the top (don't pull it tight when you stitch the row), as this will stop the stitches from getting tight and not lying flat. If you need to re-thread your needle with new thread it is best to do this at the end of the line, so that you can finish off in the border and start a new line.

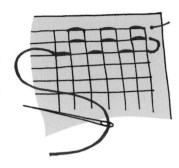

4 On the third line start the row by going down from the front to the back and then up again, so that the first stitch of that row is on the back. Continue along the line. If you follow the stitch guide on page 122 it all becomes very clear as you start stitching.

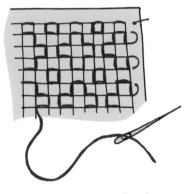

5 The fourth line repeats line three—these four lines make up the pattern. Working in groups of two lines, alternate the stitch position every two lines to continue to the end. Now you repeat the whole thing for the vertical lines. Starting in the top right corner, make your first stitch by going down from the front to the back. Continue stitching as you did on the horizontal lines and you will soon see the pattern emerging.

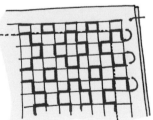

6 When you have finished the stitching, place the back and front pieces with right sides together and pin in position. Sew a line of machine stitches around the grid—I always make the seam one square in. Leave a gap of about 2¾ in. (7 cm) along one edge.

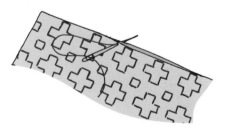

7 Trim back the seam allowance all around to about ⅓ in. (8 mm). Turn the coaster the right way out, fold in the raw edges at the gap, and sew closed with small stitches. Press the coaster. If you used a heat-erasable pen the lines will magically disappear. If you used an air-erasable pen, the lines will fade away.

THOUGHTFUL GIFTS

EMBROIDERED SHIRT

LITTLE ACORN COVERED BUTTONS

TASSELED TREE DECORATIONS

SPLATTER TOTE BAG

DOODLE NOTEBOOKS

BORO STITCHED JEANS

KNOT STITCHED LINEN BAG

SOFT LEATHER POUCHES

WAVE STITCHED CRAFT BAG

RAINBOW-HANDLED STRING BAG

FLORAL NEEDLEPOINT CARDS

EMBROIDERED SHIRT

Transform a plain white shirt into a unique and beautiful item of clothing with some delicate embroidery. With this kind of embroidery, you don't have to follow the pattern to the exact stitch; you may even want to use the outline and fill it in with your own ideas and design. **FOLLOW YOUR HEART** and see what happens. It also doesn't matter if some of your stitch work is a little wobbly—it is all part of the charm and character of handstitched pieces— so **RELAX** and **LET GO OF ANY JUDGMENTS**.

YOU WILL NEED

Template on page 121

Tracing paper

Masking tape

Sharp pencil or air-eraseable fabric pen

Scissors

Small embroidery hoop (optional)

Stranded embroidery floss (thread) in assorted colors

Needle

NOTES I don't often use embroidery hoops as I find it easier without one, but it is a case of preference—you may find that having the fabric pulled taut is helpful.

1 Transfer the design of the bird from the template on page 121 onto tracing paper.

2 I used a lightbox to transfer the design onto the shirt but if you haven't got a one you can stick the design to the window with some sticky tape and place the shirt over the top. Use a sharp pencil or air-eraseable pen to transfer the design onto the fabric. (Alternatively you could cut out the bird and draw around it, filling in other details by hand.)

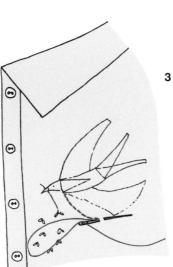

3 Secure the fabric in an embroidery hoop, if using. Start with the outline of the bird: use two strands of embroidery floss (thread) and whipped backstitch (see page 10) to stitch the complete outline of the bird.

4 Follow the stitch template on page 121 to fill in the design, using whipped backstitch, straight stitch, bullion knots, and detached chain stitches (see the Techniques section on pages 10–11 for more information on how to work these stitches).

LITTLE ACORN COVERED BUTTONS

Making covered buttons is a wonderful way to show off small pieces of embroidery. When you realize how **EASY** they are to make, it becomes quite addictive. It is so **SATISFYING** to clip the back in place, turn the button over and reveal such a perfectly covered, charming button. I have created a simple acorn design and used different colored scraps of fabric and embroidery thread to make this cheerfully vibrant collection.

YOU WILL NEED

Scraps of fabric–cotton and linen fabrics that aren't too heavy work best

Scissors

Template and stitch guide on page 120

Tracing paper

Small embroidery hoop (optional)

Six-stranded embroidery floss (thread)

Embroidery needle

Self cover buttons, about 1¼ in. (3 cm) in diameter

1 Cut out several scraps of fabric that are about 4 in. (10 cm) square. This is larger than you need but it is much easier to embroider on a larger piece. If you have a small embroidery hoop and want to use it, you will need to cut scraps of fabric to the size of your hoop with at least 1¼ in. (3 cm) extra all round. Use the templates on page 120 to trace out the acorn designs and transfer the designs onto the fabric (see page 8), making sure you position the design in the center of the fabric piece.

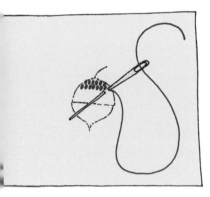

2 Divide the six strands of embroidery thread into groups of two strands. The acorns are made up using three different stitches: whipped backstitch, bullion knots and straight stitches (see Techniques on pages 10–11). Follow the stitch guide to embroider the designs.

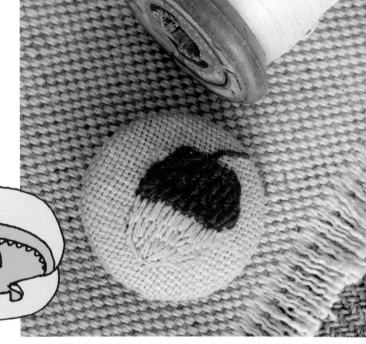

3 Cut out a circle from the fabric, making sure that the acorn design is centered and that you have enough fabric to go over the side of the button and tuck into the teeth around the under rim. Place the fabric over the front section of the self-cover button part. Making sure that the acorn design stays centered, pull the fabric around the edge, tucking it under at the back so it attaches to the small teeth, all around the under rim. If you find there is too much fabric, you can trim it a little, although if you have chosen a fine fabric you should be fine.

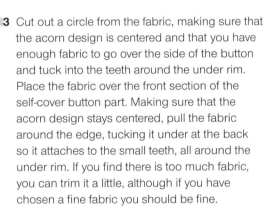

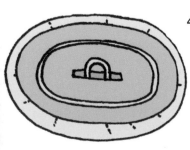

4 Snap the back of the self-cover button in place to complete. If your fabric is a little bulky you may need a small hammer to tap it into place, but if your fabric is thin, it should just snap on.

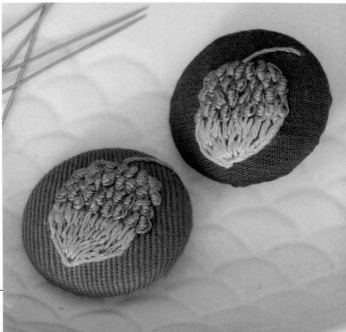

TASSELED TREE DECORATIONS

Decorating the tree at Christmas is always the part of the festive preparations I look forward to the most. Many of the decorations on our Christmas tree are homemade and it is always a joy to unpack these little ornaments year after year. Christmas can be a time for **REFLECTION** and so many of these decorations hold **MEMORIES**. These rainbow bright silk thread decorations remind me of little dancing figures or angels as they twist and turn among the green foliage. The metal parts are D rings but if you can't find them, you could buy some cheap hoop earrings in different sizes instead. I used embroidery floss (thread) to make mine, but you have to separate the six strands, so it is better to use brightly colored sewing thread. If you do use embroidery floss, the single strand is thicker than sewing thread, so you do not have to wrap it around quite as many times.

YOU WILL NEED
(FOR 1 DECORATION)

Two pieces of card: 3½ in. (8 cm) and 1½ in. (4 cm) wide

Embroidery floss (thread) or sewing thread (you need thin thread that you would use with a sewing machine) in assorted colors

Scissors

Two D rings: 3½ in. (8.5 cm) and 1½ in. (4 cm)

Masking tape

Embroidery floss (thread) or similar to hang the finished ornament

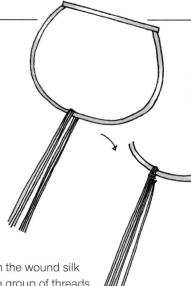

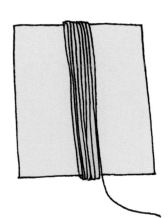

1 Take the larger of the two pieces of card and a reel of silk thread. Wind the thread around the card about 60–90 times.

2 Cut through the wound silk and fold the group of threads over the large D ring. Take a length of silk, bunch the threads tightly together at the top and wind the thread around a few times. Secure with a knot and cut the ends off to roughly the same length as the main threads.

3 Repeat to make a total of 11 knots, working out from the center knot and changing the colors as you like (I used just three colors on the large ring). Now repeat with the smaller ring, winding the thread around the smaller card. I put just three sections of thread on this one.

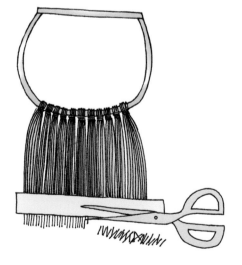

4 Take the larger ring, smooth the threads down, and bunch the top bits close together. Position a piece of masking tape across the loose ends and then cut across with a sharp pair of scissors to give the ends a nice clean line (I made my threads 2½ in. (6 cm) in length).

5 Do the same for the small D ring, this time cutting the threads to about ¾ in. (2 cm). If you want the threads to be super smooth you can finish them off with a few strokes with some hair straighteners. Tie the two D rings together with a length of embroidery floss (thread) to hang on the tree.

SPLATTER TOTE BAG

I have a serving dish that I bought in a Spanish market with a glazed splatter pattern. It is one of my favorite plates and I thought the pattern would look great on a bag too. The actual splatter painting was really **FUN**—it's a wonderful **FREEING** feeling to be let loose with a pot of colored dye and a length of fabric. Make sure you do this outside or, if you are inside, make sure you protect the area with lots of newspaper! It is best to make a bigger piece of fabric than you need, so that you can select the best area of pattern. Any leftovers can be kept for other projects, or make some bags to give as gifts for your friends. I have added a small tag, in a contrasting color, on one side of the bag.

NOTE
Adding a small tag in a contrasting color is a little extra detail that looks a bit like a designer label and makes the bag look even more special. The unexpected zing of color cheers me up whenever I see it.

YOU WILL NEED

Fabric dye—I used navy blue

Old paintbrush

1 yard (1 m) canvas or thick calico fabric (you won't need all of this so you can use less)

Scrap of colored fabric, 2½ x 2 in. (6 x 5 cm)

Scissors

Needle and matching sewing thread

10 in. (25 cm) leather strip, about ¾ in. (1.5 cm) wide

Leather hole punch

Pencil

Stud rivets

1 Mix up the dye following the packet instructions. Place the fabric on a well protected surface, or ideally outside—I placed mine down on some grass in the garden. Use the paintbrush to flick and splatter the paint onto the fabric. I wanted the splatters to fill the bottom half of the bag, so I tried to keep the splatters to one half of the fabric.

2 Leave the fabric to dry for an hour or two and then rinse under a cold tap until the water runs clear to remove any excess dye (or follow the manufacturer's instructions). Leave to dry.

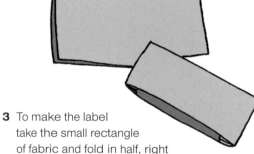

3 To make the label take the small rectangle of fabric and fold in half, right sides together, aligning the two shorter ends. Stitch down each short side with a ¼ in. (5 mm) seam allowance. Turn the right way out and press with an iron.

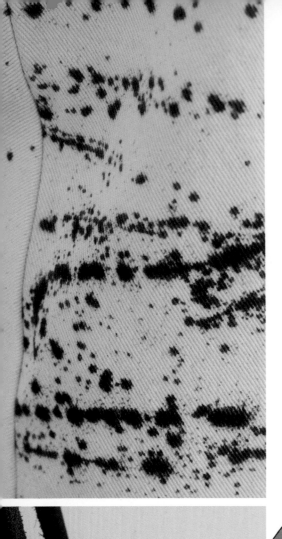

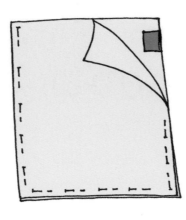

4 Cut out two rectangles of fabric from your splatter cloth, each measuring 16½ x 18½ in. (42 x 46 cm). Pin the two main pieces with right sides together, positioning the label about 3 in. (8 cm) down from the top edge on one side of the bag. The label should be on the inside of the bag with the raw edges lined up with the raw edges of the bag.

5 Stitch around the three sides of the bag with a ½ in. (1 cm) seam allowance.

6 Fold over a double ½ in. (1 cm) hem at the top edge of the bag, pin and stitch. Turn the bag the right way out and press with an iron.

7 If you have purchased some rivets to attach the handles, they often come with a punch tool to make the holes in the leather. I used my rotary hole punch that I use for paper, adjusting it to the right size for the rivets. Mark two points on the leather strip, ¾ in. (1.5 cm) and 1¼ in. (3 cm) in from one of the ends of leather. Punch out the holes at these points. Repeat on the other end and do the same on the other leather strip.

8 Position the handles on the bag—I placed mine about 4 in. (10 cm) in from each edge and so that they extended 1½ in. (4 cm) onto the bag. With a pencil mark through the holes onto the canvas.

9 Punch out the holes in the canvas and align the leather strips on the bag, matching up the holes. Follow the instructions that come with the rivets to attach the two parts, back and front, through the holes on the canvas and leather.

DOODLE NOTEBOOKS

The designs on the covers of these little notebooks are made with repeat pattern printing and freehand drawing with a fabric pen. Have you ever been talking on the phone with a pen and paper in your hand and found that the paper gets covered in doodles? Well mine does! Doodling helps to **FOCUS YOUR MIND**, channel your thoughts, and can also have a **CALMING** effect. There are no templates for these designs as it's much more fun to make up your own. Practice on paper first—just start in one corner and see where the pen takes you. It's all about **LETTING GO** and having fun!

YOU WILL NEED
(FOR 1 NOTEBOOK)

15 x 8 in. (37 x 20 cm) plain cotton fabric

15 x 8 in. (37 x 20 cm) iron-on interfacing

Iron

Erasers

Craft knife

Fabric dye stamp pad

Fabric dye pen—I used black

14 in. cotton tape, ½ in. (1 cm) wide

A piece of thin card, 10 x 7 in. (25 x 17 cm)

Rectangles of paper, 9¾ x 6¾ in. (24.5 x 16.5 cm)—I use the empty pages from old school exercise books

Cutting mat

Book binder's awl or something sharp to make a hole through the paper and card

Needle and sewing thread

1 Follow the instructions on your fusible interfacing to iron it to the wrong side of your fabric.

2 Using the craft knife, cut a shape from an eraser. It can be simple like a circle or semicircle. Use a pencil to draw out the shape first, if you find that easier.

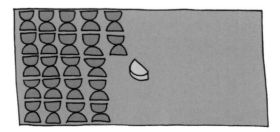

3 Print a repeating pattern with the cut shape using a fabric dye stamp pad. I like to use the same color as the fabric but a few shades darker.

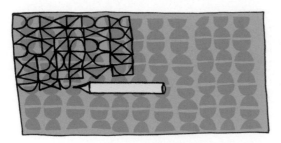

4 Use the fabric pen to draw in some patterns over the top of the repeating pattern. You can practice on some paper first or do something similar to mine.

5 Fold over a ½ in. (1 cm) hem to the wrong side all around the edges and press. Cut the cotton tape in half. Use a pin or pencil to mark the center point at each of the shorter ends of the fabric rectangle. Fold about ½ in. (1 cm) of tape over to the wrong side of the fabric where you have marked. Fold about ½ in. (1 cm) of tape over to the wrong side of the fabric where you have marked. Fold about ½ in. (1 cm) of tape over to the wrong side of the fabric where you have marked. Pin the first 2 in. (5 cm) of tape to the right side of the fabric and stitch around all the edges of the tape, where you have pinned it to the fabric. Repeat this at the other end of the fabric.

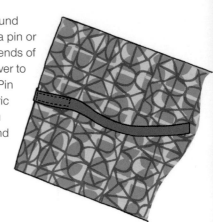

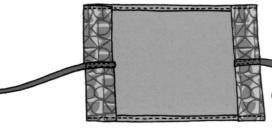

6 To make fabric pockets to slip the notebook into, fold 2 in. (5 cm) over to the wrong side at both short edges. Sew a line of stitching, close to the edge, at the top and bottom of the notebook cover. Fold the cover in half and press with an iron.

7 To make the notebook, fold the card and paper pages in half. Open up the pages and place them on top of the card, aligning the crease down the middle and making sure that there they are centered so that the card overlaps the paper evenly at the top and bottom.

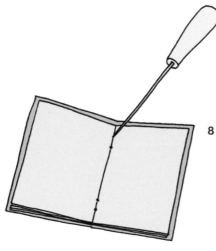

8 Use a pencil to mark points along the center crease at 1¼ in. (3 cm) and 2 in. (5 cm) in from one side. Do the same on the other end of the central crease. Use the awl and cutting mat to make holes through the layers of card and paper at these points.

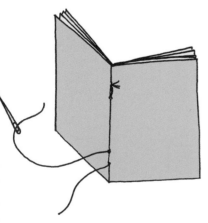

9 Thread a needle with sewing thread, doubled up for strength. Take the needle through from the front at the first hole and then back to the front through the second hole. Repeat this again and then tie off the ends with a knot. Trim the ends down to ½ in. (1 cm). Repeat this on the other set of holes.

10 Slide the card cover into the fabric pockets on either side to finish.

TAKE A MOMENT...
Mending and patching means your clothes will last longer. It's much more eco-friendly, plus they will look completely unique.

BORO STITCHED JEANS

YOU WILL NEED

An item of clothing

Small scraps of fabric

Scissors

Pins

Needle

Six-stranded embroidery floss
(thread)

Dressmaker's chalk pencil
(optional)

Boro stitching is an ancient Japanese technique of visible mending. Patches of fabric and multiple rows of small stitches are used to turn something that may have been worn out and full of holes into an original item of clothing. If you were patching a child's pair of jeans you could use scraps of fabric from clothes that they have long grown out of. As time goes on you can keep adding sections. Recycling in this way means that **CHERISHED MEMORIES** of times gone by are captured and you have created something that is truly beautiful and **ORIGINAL**. To me that is **MEANINGFUL** and **HAPPY** stitching.

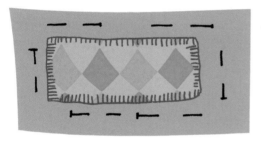

1 To sew a patch where the fabric is placed behind the rip, cut a piece of fabric from your scraps that is ½ in. (1 cm) larger all around than the hole or rip you are patching up. Place it behind the rip with the right side showing through the rip. Pin in place.

2 Thread a needle with two strands of embroidery floss (thread). Decide where you want to position your rectangle of stitches. You can stitch these rectangles of stitches by eye, or you can draw them out with a dressmaker's chalk pencil. Sew a line of running stitch down one side of your planned rectangle, making sure that you go over a section of the scrap fabric. When you sew the running stitch try to keep the space in between each stitch the same length as the actual stitch.

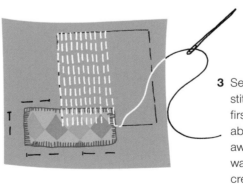

3 Sew another line of stitching next to the first, spacing this line about ⅛ in. (4 mm) away. Continue in this way until you have created a rectangle of running stitches.

4 To sew a section with a patch on the outside of the garment, cut a rectangle of fabric to the size you want. Turn in a small hem all around and press with an iron. Place the patch in position on the garment and pin in place. Repeat step 2 to create another rectangle of running stitch lines.

5 Continue making rectangles of stitches, varying the direction of the stitching and changing the color of the thread if you like.

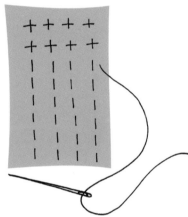

6 To make the cross-stitched sections, make the rows of running stitch as before, but space the lines about ¼ in. (5 mm) apart. Then make rows of stitching at right angles to the first rows, crossing over all the stitches in the first row.

KNOT STITCHED LINEN BAG

This simple drawstring linen bag has been transformed into something very special with a series of stitched knots in a striking and contemporary geometric pattern. It's big enough to be useful at home but not huge, making it ideal to pop into your suitcase when traveling. The stitch is a bullion knot and is one of my favorite stitches, as it is versatile and can be used in many different ways. The stitching **FOCUSES YOUR MIND** so that it becomes a **SOOTHING** and **RELAXING** occupation.

YOU WILL NEED

Template on page 121

Tracing paper and pencil

Two pieces of fabric,
30 x 17½ in. (75 x 44 cm)

3 skeins of six-stranded embroidery floss (thread) in black

3 skeins of six-stranded embroidery floss (thread) in white

Pins

2 yards (2 m) cotton cord, ⅛ in. (3 mm) in diameter

Safety pin

1 Using the template on page 121 and some tracing paper, transfer the design onto one of the pieces of fabric (for the front of the bag), choosing your preferred method (the different methods for transferring onto fabric are explained on page 8). I traced out the template and used the widow as a lightbox. Make sure the template is centered, with the base of the diamond shape 3½ in. (9cm) up from the bottom edge. Start by tracing the diamond shape in the middle of the pattern.

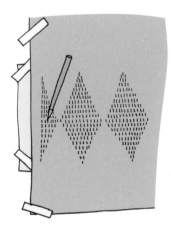

2 Now draw in the two diamond shapes either side of this first one, leaving a gap of ⅜ in. (8 mm) between the shapes and making sure that the dots are lined up. Complete the row with two half-diamond shapes on either side of the three already drawn in.

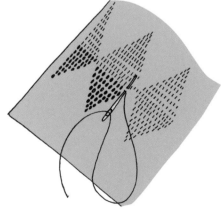

3 Using all six strands of the black embroidery floss (thread), start stitching the bullion knots at each of the marked spots on the lower half of the diamonds (see page 11). Switch to white embroidery floss (thread) to complete the design.

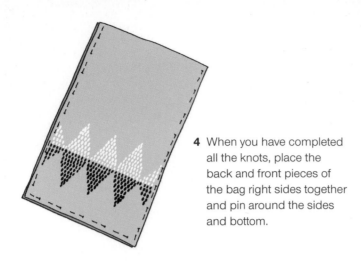

4 When you have completed all the knots, place the back and front pieces of the bag right sides together and pin around the sides and bottom.

5 Sew down one side, along the bottom and up the other side, leaving a small gap in the seam 6 in. (15 cm) down from the top, on each side. Make the gaps 1½ in. (3.5 cm) in length. Then fold over a single ½ in. (1 cm) hem all around the top. Pin and sew.

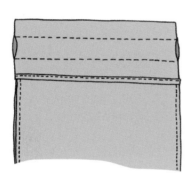

6 Fold over 4 in. (10 cm) to the wrong side all around the top. Start on the front at the top of the gap you left in the side seam and pin across one side of the bag, in a straight line to the top of the gap on the other side of the bag. Continue pinning round on the back of the bag until you are back where you started. Sew a line of stitching, marked where the pins are. Repeat to pin and stitch around the bottom of the gap, again starting at the side edge. Turn the bag the right way out and press.

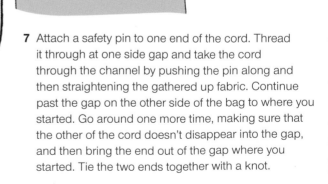

7 Attach a safety pin to one end of the cord. Thread it through at one side gap and take the cord through the channel by pushing the pin along and then straightening the gathered up fabric. Continue past the gap on the other side of the bag to where you started. Go around one more time, making sure that the other of the cord doesn't disappear into the gap, and then bring the end out of the gap where you started. Tie the two ends together with a knot.

SOFT LEATHER POUCHES

These striking zipped leather pouches are so useful. I always carry a pencil case and notebook with me so I can jot down ideas or design patterns wherever I am. It keeps me occupied, especially on long train journeys. **DRAWING REPEAT PATTERNS** and doodling **CALMS** and **FOCUSES THE MIND**, no matter what may be going on. You could make up your own patterns to go on these smart, leather pouches, which would also make very good cases to hold a small travel sewing kit. There is plenty of room for a small pair of scissors, needles, thread and the project, for embroidery on the go!

YOU WILL NEED

Black fabric paint

Black fabric marker

Two rectangles of soft, thin leather, each 10 x 4½ in. (25 x 11.5 cm) for the large pouch or 5½ x 4 in. (14 x 10 cm) for the small pouch

Scissors

Scrap of soft, thin leather

A small scrap of leather

Zipper that is about 1 in. (2.5 cm) longer than the leather piece (you can cut it from a continuous zipper)

Sewing machine fitted with a leather needle

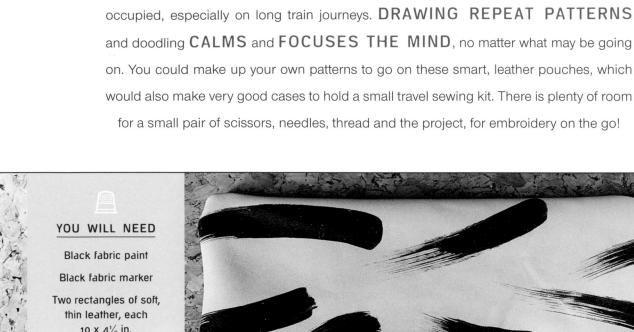

NOTE
The small pouch is made in exactly the same way. I left out the small strips of leather across the ends of the zipper, but you can include them if you want.

Using the fabric paint and fabric marker, create your design on the leather. I used simple brushstrokes for the large pouch and lines of dashes made with the nib shape of the pen on the small pouch. Don't worry if the lines go wobbly of you don't make the dash marks evenly spaced, those imperfections are what gives a pattern its character.

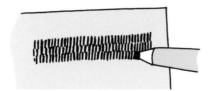

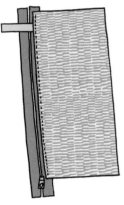

2 Cut two small strips of leather from your scrap piece, measuring ½ x 2 in. (1 x 5 cm). Lay the zipper down on a flat surface, with the top of the zipper facing towards you. Place one of the leather rectangles face upward onto the right-hand side of the zipper. Position the metal clipped end of the zipper ¾ in. (2 cm) from the end of the leather piece.

Place a thin strip of leather across the zip at each end, covering the metal end clip. Tuck the ends of the strips under the leather rectangle by about ¾ in. (2 cm). Pin in position. Using a zipper foot, machine stitch along the top edge of the leather rectangle. Keep your stitching close to the zipper teeth but not too close that the zipper gets stuck.

3 Place the other leather rectangle onto the left-hand side of the zipper in the same way. Tuck the strips under the left rectangle as you did on the other side. Pin and stitch in position again making sure the zipper pull will still move freely along the zipper.

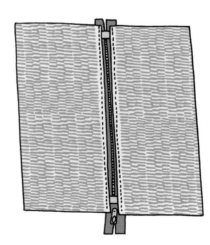

4 Turn the pouch inside out, so that the right (patterned) sides are together. Pin down the two sides and along the base. Open up the zipper to about two-thirds of the length. Sew down the sides and along the base with a ⅓ in. (8 mm) seam allowance. You will be sewing over the zipper teeth at the top, which you can do, but I always go very slowly at this point.

5 Trim off the ends of the zipper. Trim back the seam to ¼ in. (5 mm) and trim the corners, making sure you don't go too close to the stitched seam. Turn the right way out.

WAVE STITCHED CRAFT BAG

This striking 3D wave pattern is made using the technique of fabric manipulation. When I am not working with fabric and textiles, paper folding is a particular love of mine, so the fact that you can combine paper-folding skills with fabric has always held a fascination for me. It looks as if it would be so complicated to make but it is much easier than it looks. As with many of the projects, it is the **RHYTHM** and **REPEAT** actions that are mindful. You become **ABSORBED** in the folding, sewing, and pressing of the fabric, while your mind is doing the opposite and is being smoothed out.

YOU WILL NEED

One piece of main fabric:
15¼ x 12 in. (38 x 30 cm)

One piece of main fabric:
15¼ x 21½ in. (38 x 54 cm)

Two pieces of main fabric:
10½ x 3½ in. (26 x 8.5 mm)

Two pieces of lining fabric:
15¼ x 12 in. (38 x 30 cm)

Air- or heat-erasable pen

Long ruler

Sewing machine

Black sewing thread and
needle

Iron

Sewing thread to
match fabric

Wooden handles with a
5¼ in. (13 cm) opening (you
can use a different size and
adapt the handle to fit)

1 Start with the long piece of main fabric. Starting 2½ in. (6 cm) from the bottom of the short edge, mark a point using the air- or heat-erasable pen. Make eight more points, spaced 1¾ in. (4.5 cm) apart. Repeat this at the other edge of the fabric. Then starting back at the first point mark a point ¾ in. (1.5 cm) above it. Do this above all the nine points on either side of the fabric. Join the marks with lines across the width.

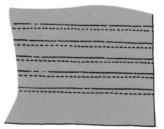

2 Starting at the bottom, sew a line of stitching across the first drawn line. I used black thread against the orange fabric, as I really wanted to emphasize the sculptural quality of the folds. Repeat this at every other line at the 1¾ in. (4.5 cm) mark. You should end up with nine sewn lines.

3 Starting with the first stitched line, fold the fabric all along the line and press with an iron. Make a line of stitching along the second drawn line. I used a color thread that matched the bag. This is the first fold. Do the same on the other lines. Fold, press, and sew. You will end up with nine folds. Press the folds so they face down toward the base of the bag.

4 Sew a line of stitching ½ in. (1 cm) in from the right edge, starting at the top sewn line down to end of the bottom fold.

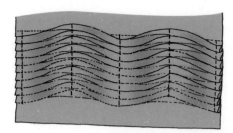

5 Measure 3½ in. (9 cm) along from right-hand side. Push all the folds so they are going in the opposite direction. Pin and sew a line of stitching from the top to the bottom of the folds. Measure 3½ in. (9 cm) from this line, push the folds so that they are facing down, pin, and sew. Repeat two more times, each time pushing the folds in the opposite direction.

6 Take the back section of the bag and place over the front section you have just made, with right sides together along the bottom and side edges; pin in position. Trim off any extra fabric from the front folded piece, so that they are the same size. Sew down each side and across the base with a ½ in. (1 cm) seam allowance. Trim back the seams to ¼ in. (5 mm).

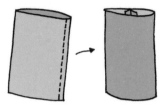

7 Take the two smaller pieces of main fabric for the handles. With right sides together, fold one of the rectangles in half down the shorter side. Sew a line of stitching ½ in. (1 cm) in from the edge. Turn the right way out and press flat with the seam centered at the back. Repeat this with the other handle section.

8 Take the two lining pieces. With right sides together, align all the edges and pin down each of the shorter sides and the bottom. Sew down each side and along the base with a ½ in. (1 cm) seam allowance, leaving a gap of about 8 in. (20 cm) along the bottom.

9 Place the fabric handle sections through the wooden handles, making sure that the seam is on the inside, and fold them in half. Place one on each right side of the bag. They should be centered, facing down with the tops aligned with the top of the bag. Pin and tack in place.

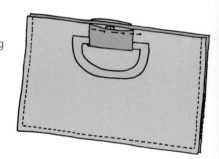

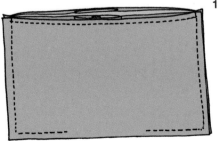

10 With the main bag turned the right way out and the lining turned inside out, slip the lining over the main bag, which means they will be right sides together. Align the top edges and pin, making sure that the side seams of the lining match the side seams of the main bag. Sew all around with a ½ in. (1 cm) seam allowance, then trim the seam down to ¼ in. (5 mm). Turn the bag the right way out by pulling the main bag though the gap in the bottom of the lining. Fold in the raw edges in the gap in the lining and sew together with small stitches. Push the lining down into the bag to finish.

RAINBOW-HANDLED STRING BAG

Macramé is a craft that has made a comeback in the last few years. Beautiful and exciting pieces can be created from, rope, string, and knots. It also fits in very well with the mindfulness concept—it requires some **CONCENTRATION**, but not too much, and it is the **REPETITIVE ACTION** of tying the knots in a sequence that is so soothing. I wanted to make something useful so I made a string bag. The basic string is from a hardware store and I used up scraps of embroidery floss (thread) that I unwound from the tangle in my sewing box (a very mindful half-hour in itself!). I was very pleased with the results and amazed at how easy it was to make.

YOU WILL NEED

A ball of soft cotton string

Scissors

A bottle

Sewing thread

Six-stranded embroidery floss (thread) in different colors

Needle

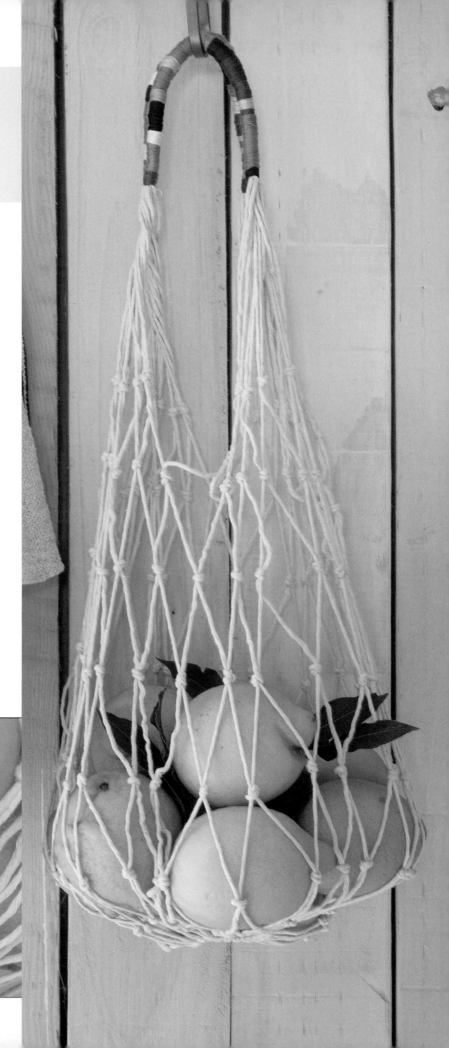

1 Cut 24 lengths of string, each 63 in. (1.6 m) in length. If you measure the first length, you can use this to cut the rest.

2 Take one of the strands and fold it in half. Tie a knot just up from the fold so that you have made a loop about 1¼ in. (3 cm) in diameter.

3 Take another length of string and fold it in half. Place the folded end under the circle of string and take the two ends of string through the loop to secure. Repeat this with all the remaining lengths of string, pushing them together as you go around the circle, so that they fit together snugly.

4 Place the ring of string over a bottle, as this makes it easier to work with. Take one right-hand length of string from a folded length and the string immediately next to it (the left-hand length of string). Tie a knot 1¼ in. (3 cm) from the ring. Move along and repeat with the next two lengths of string, trying to place the knot at the same level. Continue all around the ring, until all the string lengths have been knotted together.

5 Move on to the next row. Repeat step 4, taking one left-hand string and one right-hand and tying a knot—this time make the length between the first knot 1½ in. (4 cm). From now on make each new row 40mm below the previous one. Continue going round and round until the last row is about 13 in. (33 cm) from the starting ring.

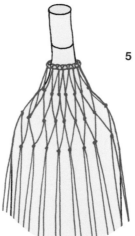

6 Trim the ends so that they are of similar lengths. Divide the strands into four equal groups. Take two of the groups, that are next to each other, overlap the cut ends by about 1¼ in. (3 cm) and tightly wrap some sewing thread around a few times before tying in a knot to secure. For extra strength you could machine stitch across this point a few times.

7 Start wrapping the colored embroidery floss (thread) around in sections. Lay about 1 in. (2.5 cm) of the floss along the handle, then wind over this strand. When you have the length you want, thread a needle through the end of the thread and take the needle back through the handle under the wound sections, coming up a few centimeters along. Pull the thread though and snip off the excess thread. Continue winding sections of colored thread along the handle, starting a new color each time in the same way. When you come to last section snip off any bits of thread that protrude from the wound section.

8 Repeat steps 6 and 7 to make the other handle. I made the colored section about 8 in. (20 cm) long.

FLORAL NEEDLEPOINT CARDS

Small needlepoint projects make wonderful greetings cards. The lucky recipient will feel very **SPECIAL** and appreciate the **CARE** that you have put into every stitch. All hand sewing is a good way to **UNWIND** and needlepoint especially so. You can get into a **STEADY RHYTHM** of stitching which is very soothing. These cards are also great fun to make and it's so satisfying to see the design develop as you stitch. I have chosen lots of vibrant colors, but you can choose any color scheme you like.

YOU WILL NEED

Template on page 120

3½ x 4½ in. (9 x 11 cm) piece of 14-count Aida fabric

Six-stranded embroidery floss (thread)

Needle

Two pieces of card: 9 x 7¼ in. (23 x 18.5 cm) and 4½ x 7¼ in. (11.5 x 18.5 cm)

Something to score the card with (the blunt side of a cutlery knife works well)

Ruler and pencil

Craft knife

Cutting mat

Glue stick

1 Trace out the design from the template on page 120 Use your preferred method to transfer the design onto the Aida fabric (see page 8). I used the window as lightbox method. Stitch the design onto the fabric, following steps 1–2 of the Abstract Framed Needlepoint project on page 96. Start ½ in. (1 cm) in from the top left.

2 When you have finished the design, sometimes you find the cloth has become slightly distorted. You can rectify this by following the instructions on page 97 but as this piece of needlepoint is quite small it should not have distorted too much.

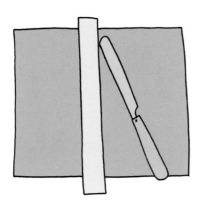

3 To make the larger card, score down the center of the larger rectangle of card; find the center by measuring the top and bottom of the card. Line the ruler up to these two marks and score down the length of the card. Fold the rectangle in half down the scored line, then open it out again.

4 Use your ruler and pencil to mark out a rectangle measuring 2½ x 3½ in. (6.5 x 8.5 cm) on the front of the card; position the rectangle 1½ in. (4 cm) from the top and centered in from each edge. Use the ruler and craft knife to cut out the section of card, positioning the card on a cutting mat.

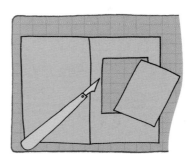

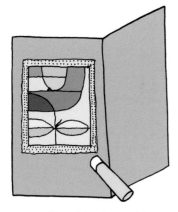

5 On the inside of the front of the card, glue all around the edge of the cut-out section, then position the needlepoint right side down so that the stitched area fits neatly into the cut-out rectangle. Press down to secure.

6 Using the glue stick, apply glue the other rectangle of card and place it down over the needlepoint on the inside front of the card. Press down to secure. It should have been cut slightly smaller than the measurement of the front, but if any bits are sticking out, trim these with the ruler and craft knife.

> **NOTE**
> The smaller card is made in exactly the same way but using smaller pieces of card: 9 x 5¾ in. (23 x 14.5 cm) and 4½ x 5¾ in. (11.5 x 14.5 cm). Position the opening 1 in. (2.5 cm) down from the top edge.

TACTILE GIFTS
FOR KIDS

LEAPING HORSE SOFTIE

SCALLOP EDGED BABY QUILT

NORDIC CHRISTMAS STOCKINGS

MINI MENAGERIE PIN BADGES

RAINDROP CLOUD MOBILE

FLUFFY KOALA BAG

SQUEEZY KITTY

LEAPING HORSE SOFTIE

Life can be so hectic. We rush around, always against the clock, and are bombarded by technology. Sometimes it is good to **CLOSE THE DOOR** on that world and **SPEND** some **QUIET TIME** to yourself, and what better way than by crafting. You'll need to use a sewing machine to make this adorable soft toy, but that can still be **MINDFUL**. Taking it slowly and methodically following the instructions step-by-step is calming and relaxing. The finished horse is **SOOTHING** to stroke. It can be enlarged to make an unusual pillow for a child's bedroom.

YOU WILL NEED

Tracing paper and pencil

Templates on page 124

20 in. (50 cm) square of cotton fabric

Pins

Scissors

7 x 8 in. (17 x 20 cm) piece of contrasting fabric (I used some faux fur)

Matching sewing thread

Sewing machine

Soft toy stuffing

Linen or jute twine (for the mane and tail)

Stranded embroidery floss (thread)

Embroidery needle

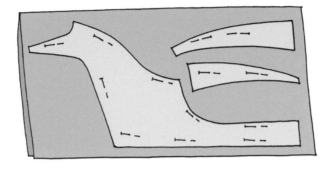

1 Trace the templates on page 124, tracing the leg piece twice. With right sides together, fold the main fabric in half. Pin all the templates to the fabric and cut out the pieces. Unpin the leg templates and pin these to the remaining folded scraps of fabric. Cut them out. You should now have two main body sections and eight leg sections (four front and four back).

2 Fold the smaller piece of fabric in half right sides together. Pin the template for the back pieces to the fabric and cut them out.

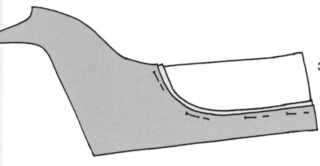

3 With right sides together, pin one back section to one main body piece. Sew together with a ½ in. (1 cm) seam, then trim back the seam to ⅛ in. (4 mm). Repeat to make the other side.

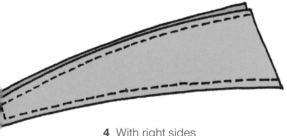

4 With right sides together, pin and stitch two leg sections together with a ½ in. (1 cm) seam. Trim back to ⅛ in. (4 mm).

5 Turn the leg the right way out—you may need something to push out the thin section at the end (I use the wooden handle of a small paintbrush). Fill the leg with the stuffing—again a paintbrush handle will help get the filling to the end. It is best to do tiny bits of stuffing at a time for an even fill. Leave ½ in. (1 cm) empty at the top of each leg. Repeat to make four legs in total.

6 To make the tassels for the mane, cut several 2½ in. (6 cm) lengths of twine. Fold a few together in half and tie some colored embroidery floss (thread) around the bottom to secure. Trim the colored thread to the same length as the twine. I used a different color for each tassel as it adds a nice detail. Make seven of these.

7 The tail tassel is made in the same way with 14 in. (35 cm) lengths of twine. This time, for a decorative detail, wind the embroidery floss around a few times at the top before tying off. I wound two sections of different colored thread around the tail.

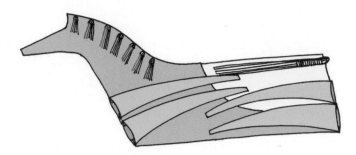

8 With the right side facing up, place the main body piece on a flat surface. Position the legs facing in with the seams aligned with the seam of the main body. The curve of the legs should be facing down, as in the diagram. Position the tassels and tail facing in, as in the diagram.

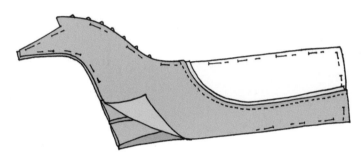

9 Place the other side of the horse section on top of this piece, with the right side facing down. Pin carefully all around, making sure that all the legs and tassels are securely pinned.

10 Sew all around with a ½ in. (1 cm) seam, leaving a gap along the underside edge of about 4 in. (10 cm).

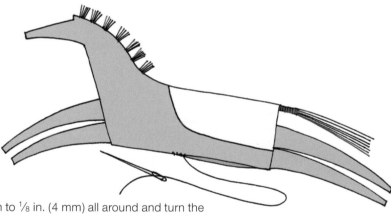

11 Trim back the seam to ⅛ in. (4 mm) all around and turn the horse the right way out. Stuff the horse with the toy stuffing, starting in the nose area and working down. Turn in the raw edges at the gap and sew up with some small slipstitches. Trim the tail and mane if they need it.

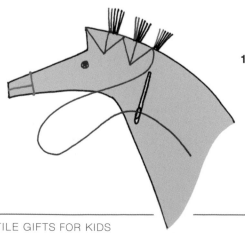

12 Embroider the pattern next to the mane with some straight stitches (see page 10). Start by taking the needle into the body of the horse away from where you want to make the first stitch. Bring the needle up at the right point but don't pull the end of the thread through, leave it in the middle of the horse. This way you won't have any visible knots. Make a bullion knot for the eye (see page 11) and stitch the mouth section.

SCALLOP EDGED BABY QUILT

This pretty pastel baby blanket is made from a Pashmina wrap I had been given as a gift; lovely as it was it's not really a color I wear. It is the softest of wool, ideal for a baby and when folded in half, exactly the right size. I used bamboo cotton wadding, as it is beautifully **SOFT** and **PLIABLE**. I finished the quilt with hand-tied embroidery threads in different colors, which add a charming detail. The finished quilt feels very special and would make a wonderful gift for a new baby and one that would be cherished for many years to come.

YOU WILL NEED

Template on page 117

Paper and pencil

Scissors

Four pieces of fabric in different colors for the scallops, each about 32 x 6 in. (80 x 15 cm)

Needle and matching sewing thread

Iron

Two rectangles of fabric, each 26 x 36 in. (65 x 90 cm)

26 x 36 in. (65 x 90 cm) bamboo cotton wadding

Six-stranded embroidery floss (thread) in assorted colors

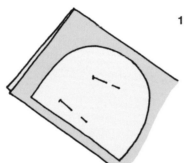

1 Trace out the template for the scallop shape. Fold one of your small lengths of fabric in half, pin the template to the fabric and cut out the shape. Repeat this three times so that you have four pairs of scallop shapes. Repeat this on the other three pieces of colored fabric to give you 16 pairs of scallop shapes.

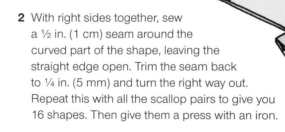

2 With right sides together, sew a ½ in. (1 cm) seam around the curved part of the shape, leaving the straight edge open. Trim the seam back to ¼ in. (5 mm) and turn the right way out. Repeat this with all the scallop pairs to give you 16 shapes. Then give them a press with an iron.

3 Take one of the lengths of main fabric. Place and pin eight of the scallop shapes, two of each color, along the top edge of the right side of the fabric. The scallops should be facing inward with the straight edge aligned with the edge of the fabric.

Pin a scallop at each end first, positioning them about ½ in. (1 cm) in from each edge. Add the rest, in a line between these two, randomly positioning the different colors. Repeat at the other end of the quilt with the remaining eight scallop shapes.

4 With right sides together, place the other main piece of fabric on top of the first, aligning all the sides and sandwiching the scallops between the two. Place the wadding on top, aligning the sides, and pin all three layers together.

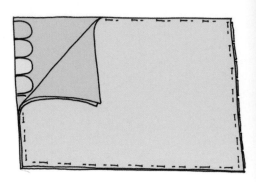

5 Sew a ½ in. (1 cm) seam all around the four sides of the quilt, leaving a gap of about 8 in. (20 cm) along one of the long edges.

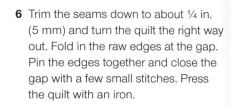

6 Trim the seams down to about ¼ in. (5 mm) and turn the quilt the right way out. Fold in the raw edges at the gap. Pin the edges together and close the gap with a few small stitches. Press the quilt with an iron.

7 I used the hand tying method to finish off the quilt and secure the three layers of fabric together. Starting at the top left of the quilt, measure 4 in. (10 cm) down from between the first and second scallop. Thread a needle with two strands of embroidery floss (thread). Take the needle down from the top at this point and then back up again, about $\frac{1}{16}$ in. (2 mm) away. Unthread the needle and tie off the two ends with three knots. Trim the ends down to ½ in. (1 cm). Continue along the width of the quilt, using the scallops as spacers.

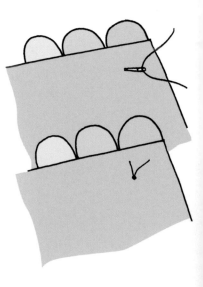

8 Do exactly the same at the other end of the quilt. Once you have these two lines finished you can use these knots to guide where you place the remaining knots. It works out that you make a new line of knots about every 6 in. (15 cm). Don't worry too much about getting the measurements exact; it won't matter if the lines are not even.

NORDIC CHRISTMAS STOCKINGS

love Chistmas, but less so those hectic days just before, when time seems to speed up and there is so much that needs doing. That is when you need to **STEP BACK**, **SET ASIDE** some time **FOR YOURSELF**, and enjoy a few hours of mindful crafting. Wrapped carefully in tissue and put away after the holiday season is over, this stocking can come out year after year. The measurements and main instructions are for the heart motif stocking. The other stocking is worked in the same way—the small circles are made from the punched-out shapes from the hole punch. As in the heart motif, the holes in the center of the flower motif start off bigger at the bottom and get smaller further up the sides.

YOU WILL NEED

Template on page 126

Paper and pencil

Scissors

18½ x 24 in. (46 x 60 cm) main fabric (I used a heavyweight cream cotton)

Transfer paper for dark fabrics

9 x 9 in. (22 x 22 cm) navy felt

Pinking shears

Hole punch–I use an adjustable rotary hole punch

Needle and cotton sewing thread to match the felt

Six-stranded embroidery floss (thread) in navy and cream

Pins

6 in. (15 cm) ribbon, ½ in. (1 cm) wide)

8 x 16½ in. (20 x 42 cm) contrasting patterned fabric

1 Enlarge the template on page 126 to the correct size and cut the template out. Fold the main fabric in half, pin the template onto it, and cut out the shape to make the front and back of the stocking.

2 Trace out the design for the felt decoration. Because these will be cut from dark fabric, you will need to use transfer paper (see page 8 for more information about the different methods of transferring patterns to fabric).

3 Follow the instructions on your transfer paper or refer to my instructions and cut out the pieces from the navy felt, using pinking shears where there are small zigzag lines on the design. Put them to one side until needed.

4 Use the hole punch to punch the holes in the triangle border section and the center of the heart design. On the center piece of the heart design I have adjusted the size of the holes, starting with bigger holes at the bottom and changing to smaller sized holes toward the top. It isn't essential, but if you have an adjustable hole punch, it adds to the detail.

5 Take the front section of the stocking and pin the felt pieces onto it, positioning the triangle border 1 in. (2.5 cm) from the top edge and the heart motif 1 in. (2.5 cm) below the border. Use dark navy cotton thread and small stitches all around the different sections to attach the felt pieces to the stocking.

6 Using two strands of cream embroidery floss (thread), stitch a line of running stitch around the center of the outer heart shape. Then complete a row of bullion knots (see page 11) all around the edge of the outer heart shape, spacing each knot about ½ in. (1 cm) apart.

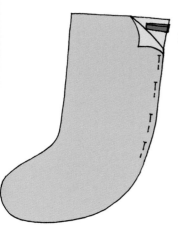

7 Take the front and back of the stocking and with right sides together pin down the long side. Take the ribbon, fold it in half, and tuck it in, so that the loop is on the inside and the ends are aligned with the edges of the stocking. It should be positioned about ¾ in. (1.5 cm) down from the top edge. Sew down this straight side, with a ½ in. (1 cm) seam allowance, stopping when you get to the beginning of the curve.

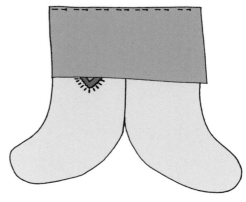

8 Lay the stocking down so that it is opened out, flat. With right sides together, pin the rectangle of contrasting fabric to the top edge of the joined stocking pieces. Sew along this edge with a ½ in. (1 cm) seam allowance.

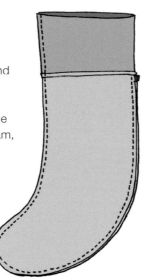

9 With right sides together, fold the stocking in half, so that the front and back align. Continue the line of stitching from where you stopped at the curve and stich all around the stocking and up the other side seam, continuing the stitching to join the contrasting border fabric too.

10 Turn over a ½ in. (1 cm) hem all along the top edge of the border piece and press. Fold over the border fabric so that the hem comes to just below the seam that joins the border to the main stocking fabric. Secure in place by stitching all around with small hand stitches.

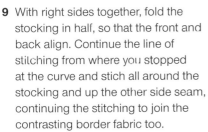

TAKE A MOMENT...
Felt is a wonderful material as it doesn't fray, which is very useful. Using the hole punch is a simple, satisfying activity, and can be calming if you're feeling a bit stressed by the holiday season.

11 Turn the stocking the right way out and press.

MINI MENAGERIE PIN BADGES

Small pieces of embroidery are **FUN** to make and very **PORTABLE**. A scrap of cloth, some thread, a needle, and small scissors and you are good to go. If you have quite a busy life, little ideas like this are perfect for when you have a few moments. I have even been known to stitch while waiting for an appointment at the dentist. This is when you can really **BENEFIT** from **MINDFUL CRAFTING**. I have made these three little creatures into these cute pin badges, but you could also sew them on as patches to transform a plain pair of jeans into something very individual and special.

YOU WILL NEED

Templates and stitch guides
on page 122

Tracing or transfer paper

Pencil

Scissors

Scraps of fabric, about
5 x 5 in. (12.5 x 12.5 cm)

Small embroidery hoop
(optional)

Six-stranded embroidery
floss (thread)

Needle

Brooch pin backs with
stitching holes

1 Trace out the templates on page 122 and use your preferred method to transfer the design onto the fabric (see page 8), making sure that you place the image in the center of the fabric. If you are using a small embroidery hoop your fabric pieces will need to be the size of your hoop with an extra 1¼ in. (3 cm) all around.

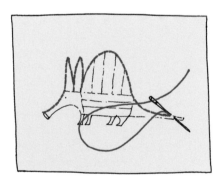

2 Follow the stitch guide to embroider the designs, using two strands of the embroidery floss (thread). I use three stitches: whipped backstitch, straight stitch and bullion knots (see pages 10–11 for stitch techniques). I find it easiest to start with the outline and then move on to the details. When you have finished with one color, finish off the end on the back of the fabric and move onto the next color.

3 You need two fabric shapes for each badge so place the embroidered piece and a plain piece of fabric right sides together and pin. Use the cutting guidelines on the template to cut out the shapes.

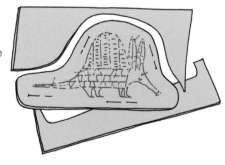

TAKE A MOMENT...
It's great to have a project like this tucked away in your bag to take out on a long journey. Once you start stitching you become immersed in the process and the hustle, bustle, and sometimes stressful surroundings melt away.

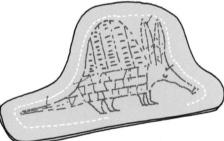

4 Sew a ½ in. (1 cm) seam around the embroidery, leaving a 1 in. (2.5 cm) gap along the straight edge at the bottom for turning.

5 Trim the seam down to about ¼ in. (5 mm) and turn the right way out. Fold in the raw edges at the gap and close up with some small stitches. Sew the brooch pin to the back of the badge.

RAINDROP CLOUD MOBILE

I do love hand stitching. It is one of the most **RELAXING** mindful crafts and when the result is this charming hanging decoration, it's all good! I have drawn up a template for the stitches on the bird, but really for an even more mindful project it is nice to **GO YOUR OWN WAY**, making it up as you go along, like stitch doodling. I have sewn mine together with a sewing machine, but if you don't have one or you don't want to use one, the felt can be stitched together by hand.

YOU WILL NEED

Templates on page 125

Tracing paper and pencil

Scissors

Pins

Felt in three colors:

7½ x 7 in. (19 x 18 cm) for the cloud

5½ x 8¾ in. (14 x 22 cm) for the bird

4¾ x 10¼ in. (12 x 26 cm) for the tree

Six-stranded embroidery floss (thread)

Needle

Air- or heat-erasable pen

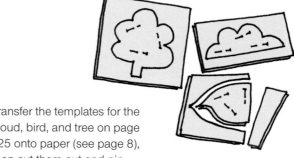

1 Transfer the templates for the cloud, bird, and tree on page 125 onto paper (see page 8), then cut them out and pin them to the felt. Cut two of each shape.

2 To embroider the raindrops onto the cloud use all six strands of the embroidery floss (thread). The drops are made using bullion knots (see page 11), stitched in rows and spaced about ¾ in. (1.5 cm) apart.

3 Cut out the shape for the bird design from the bird template and place it on the cut-out felt shape. Pin in position, leaving a border around the edge, then draw around this with an air- or heat-erasable pen. You can either stitch the design freehand or use your chosen method of transfer to place the design on the fabric (see page 8). I used two strands of embroidery floss (thread) and a combination of detached chain stitch, bullion knots and straight stitches (see pages 10–11).

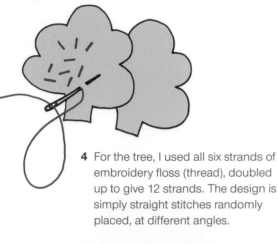

4 For the tree, I used all six strands of embroidery floss (thread), doubled up to give 12 strands. The design is simply straight stitches randomly placed, at different angles.

5 Pin the felt shapes together in their pairs. Either use a sewing machine to stitch them together, stitching about ¼ in. (5 mm) in from the edge, or hand stitch together using a small overstitch all the way around.

6 Thread a needle with some embroidery floss (thread) and tie a knot at the end. Starting at the center bottom of the tree, take the needle in between the two pieces of felt. Come out at the center of the back section, take a small stitch and carry on up through to the center top of the tree. Continue through the bird and the cloud in the same way.

7 Even out the thread between the pieces—I left a 1 in. (2.5 cm) gap. Make a loop by bringing the needle back to where the thread emerges from the center of the cloud. Secure with a few stitches. Lose the end of the thread by taking the needle into the middle and coming out on the back a few millimeters down from the top. Snip off the end of the thread.

FLUFFY KOALA BAG

The idea for this cute koala came about in a bit of a roundabout way. I always have small pieces of embroidery on the go, so that when I want to **WIND DOWN**, create something, and enjoy a few moments in **QUIET CONTEMPLATION**, it's there to pick up and enjoy. I was working a circular sample piece and when I put it down, I happened to place it down on the fluffy fabric. Straight away I thought it looked like a nose and then the idea of a koala came to me. The embroidered piece ended up as the cheeks of the koala—I was so pleased with the result!

YOU WILL NEED

Templates on page 123

Paper and pencil

Scissors

Pins

Main fluffy fabric: about 20 x 20 in. (50 x 50 cm)

Lining fabric: 20 x 16 in. (50 x 40 cm)

Scrap of black fabric for the nose (I used thin faux suede)

Scrap of plain white fabric for the cheeks (I used linen)

Needle and black embroidery floss (thread)

Sewing machine

Matching sewing thread

Two safety soft toy eyes or buttons (if the bag is for a very young child, sew the eyes)

1 yard (1 m) cotton tape, ¾ in. (1.5 cm) wide

1 Enlarge the templates on page 123 to the right size and transfer to some paper (see page 8). Cut them out. Pin the sections for the front and back, side triangles, and ears onto the reverse side of the fabric and cut out the shapes. Cut out the sections for the lining and the front of the ears in the same way. Cut out the nose section.

2 For the embroidered cheeks, you want to end up with a semicircle that measures about 2¾ in. (7 cm) across and 1¼ in. (3 cm) in diameter but it is best to sew on a larger piece of at least double that size and cut it down afterwards. Thread the needle with one strand of six-stranded embroidery floss (thread). Bring the needle up where you want to start. Using a daisy stitch (see page 10), sew a group of stitches around in a semicircle. Make a second row, keeping the rows close together with no gaps in between them. Keep adding rows until your semicircle is roughly the right size. Repeat to make a second cheek. It doesn't have to be exact, you can make them a bit bigger if you want.

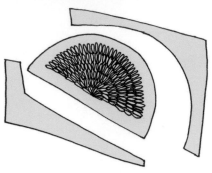

3 Trim to ½ in. (1 cm) along the base of the semicircle and ⅓ in. (8 mm) all around the curve.

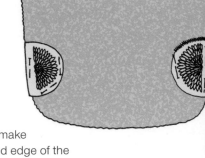

4 Place the semicircles on either side of the front section. They should be positioned about 2¾ in. (7 cm) down from the top, with the side edges aligned. Pin in place. Set your sewing machine to a close zigzag stitch and make a line of stitching all around the curved edge of the semicircle. I used the same color thread as the fabric.

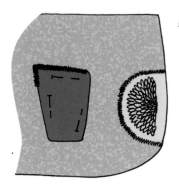

5 Position the nose in the center of the front section. Pin and stitch around with a close zigzag stitch. I used black thread.

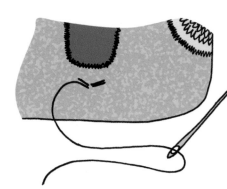

6 Embroider a mouth by stitching some straight stitches into a flattened 'V' shape. Attach the safety eyes following the instructions on the packet. If you prefer to embroider these, two bullion knots sewn close together for each eye would work well (see page 11).

7 Pin the two ear pieces with right sides together. Sew all around the curve with a ½ in. (1 cm) seam allowance. Repeat with the other ear. Trim back to ¼ in. (5 mm) and turn the right way out.

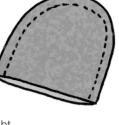

8 With right sides together, fold one of the triangle sections in half, following the fold guide on the template. Stitch with a ½ in. (1 cm) seam allowance down the straight edge that is opposite to the right-angled corner. Repeat this with the other triangular piece. Turn them the right way out and trim back the seam to ¼ in. (5 mm).

9 Take the two lining pieces and pin with right sides together. Sew all around the curved section with a ½ in. (1 cm) seam allowance, leaving the top, straight edge unstitched and a gap in the base of about 5 in. (12 cm). Trim the seams back to ¼ in. (5 mm).

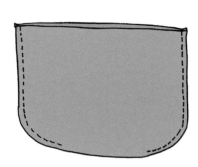

10 To assemble all the elements, place the front section face up. Position the ears, with fur side up, ¾ in. (1.5 cm) in from each side and with the raw edges aligned at the top. Place the triangles ¾ in. (1.5 cm) down from the top on each side, facing in, at right angles to the side and with the raw edges aligned. Pin all these into place and tack into position.

11 Position the back piece over the front with right sides together and pin. Sew all around the curved section with a ½ in. (1 cm) seam allowance and then turn the right way out. If you can see any tacking stitches along this seam, remove them.

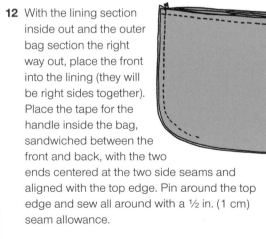

12 With the lining section inside out and the outer bag section the right way out, place the front into the lining (they will be right sides together). Place the tape for the handle inside the bag, sandwiched between the front and back, with the two ends centered at the two side seams and aligned with the top edge. Pin around the top edge and sew all around with a ½ in. (1 cm) seam allowance.

13 Turn the bag the right way out by pulling the front through the gap in the lining. Fold in the raw edges at the gap and sew it closed with small stitches. Push the lining down inside the bag. If there any visible tacking stitches at the base of the ears, cut them out.

YOU WILL NEED
(FOR 1 LARGE KITTY)

Template on page 117

Main body fabric, about
10½ x 6 in. (26 x 15 cm)

Shorts fabric, about
6½ x 6½ in. (16 x 16 cm)

Small scrap of
contrasting fabric for the
face—I used linen

Small scrap of fabric
for socks

Small scrap of fabric for
the ears

Sewing machine

Toy stuffing

Small paintbrush
(optional)

Embroidery floss
(thread) in black, pink,
and grey

YOU WILL NEED
(FOR 1 BABY KITTY)

Template on page 117

Main body fabric, about
4 x 6½ in. (10 x 16 cm)

Head fabric, about
5 x 2½ in. (12 x 6 cm)

SQUEEZY KITTY

Sometimes life feels so hectic; we are always rushing around doing things that have to be done, and it often feels like there are never enough hours in the day. To be able to **RELAX** and **WIND DOWN** from our busy schedules is important for our wellbeing. Setting up your sewing machine in a quiet corner and happily spending a few hours crafting can be a good way to **RELIEVE** any **STRESS** that may have built up. Whether it is sewing an item of clothing, a new bag, or this adorably, cute kitty, it is good to have that **"ME" TIME**. Soft toys are great fun to sew and this one would make a wonderful gift, if you can bear to part with it!

1 **To make the large kitty:** use the templates on page 117 to cut out the required number of fabric pieces for the different sections of the kitty.

2 To make the ears, pin the front and back sections right sides together. Sew together with a ½ in. (1 cm) seam allowance, leaving the straight edge open. Trim the seam allowance and turn the right way out. Press. Repeat for the other ear.

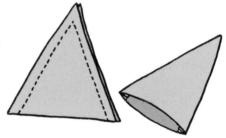

3 With right sides together pin the sock section to the leg section, along the short edge. Sew together with a ½ in. (1 cm) seam allowance. Trim the seam allowance and press the seam open. Repeat this with the other side of the leg.

4 With right sides together, pin the leg sections together. Sew around the edge, leaving the top of the leg open, with a ½ in. (1 cm) seam allowance. Trim the seam allowance and turn the right way out. Repeat this with the other leg and the two arms.

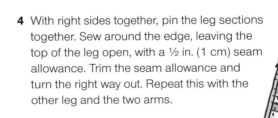

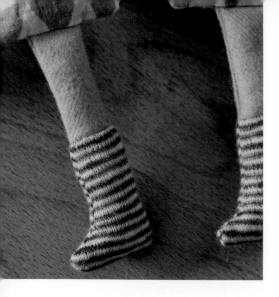

5 Stuff the legs and arms until they are firm and well shaped, making sure that the stuffing gets all the way down to the end. Use small amounts of stuffing at a time and use something like the handle of a small paintbrush, to push it down.

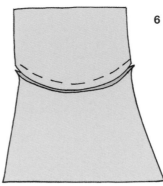

6 To make the top of the body section, pin the face and upper body right sides together. You are pinning two curves together here, so you may find it helpful to tack the seams together after pinning. Sew together with a ½ in. (1 cm) seam allowance. Trim back the seam and press the seam open.

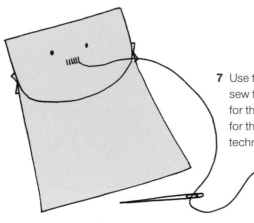

7 Use two strands of embroidery floss (thread) to sew two bullion knots for the eyes, satin stitch for the nose and cheeks, and straight stitches for the small and whiskers (see stitch techniques on pages 10–11).

8 With right sides together, pin together the top body section with the front shorts section. Sew together with a ½ in. (1 cm) seam allowance. Trim the seam allowance and press the seam open. Repeat this with the back top body and back section of shorts.

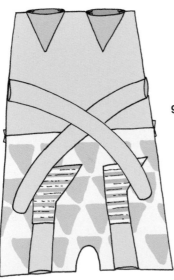

9 To assemble the kitty place the back section with right side facing upwards on a flat surface. Place the ears with the pink side facing upwards, aligning the two top seams together and positioning them ½ in. (1 cm) in from each edge. Position the arms facing into the body about 2½ in. (6 cm) down from the top edge and the legs centered along the bottom edge of the shorts and facing into the body. Tack (baste) these all into position.

10 With right sides facing, place the front section of the body on top of the back section. Pin all around the edge. Sew together with a ½ in. (1 cm) seam allowance, leaving a 2½ in. (6 cm) gap down one side of the body. Trim back the seam and turn the right way out. Stuff the body with the toy filling and then sew up the gap with some small stitches.

11 To make the baby kitty: use the templates on page 117 to cut the required number of fabric pieces for the different sections of the kitty. Follow step 6 to make the front and back sections and stitch them together.

12 Follow step 7 to embroider the eyes, nose, mouth, and whiskers.

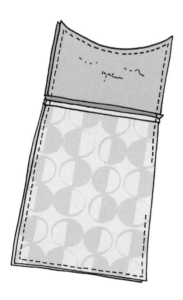

13 With right sides together pin the front and back sections together. Sew around the edge with a ½ in. (1 cm) seam allowance, leaving a 1¼ in. (3.5 cm) gap in the side seam. Trim back the seams and turn the right way out. Stuff with the toy filling and sew up the gap with small stitches.

CREATIVE WALL ART

ABSTRACT FRAMED NEEDLEPOINT
COPPER HOOP MACRAMÉ
CORAL-INSPIRED EMBROIDERY HOOPS
LEAPING TIGER WALL ART
ART DECO WALL HANGING
DELICATE FLORAL WALL HANGING
TEXTURED WEAVE

ABSTRACT FRAMED NEEDLEPOINT

There is something very **SATISFYING** about needlepoint. Watching the design develop bit by bit, with all the stitches fitting neatly together is a perfect example of **MINDFUL STITCHING**—repetitive and **MEDITATIVE**. When you place the last stitch in position, it is like placing the last piece of a jigsaw. If you are new to needlepoint, this is a perfect project to start on. It is stitched in a half cross tent stitch that is very easy to learn. I have designed a piece to frame, in pale pastel colors with one bright standout color, but choose your own palette to fit your décor. Cutting up colored paper is helpful when choosing the combination of colors or use paint swatches. If necessary, make a card mount so that the piece fits your frame.

YOU WILL NEED

Scrap of fabric to practice on

Template on page 125

7 x 9 in. (18 x 23 cm) piece of 14-count Aida fabric

Six-stranded embroidery floss (thread)—I used it doubled up to make 12 strands

Needle

Mapping pins

Wooden board

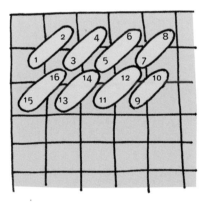

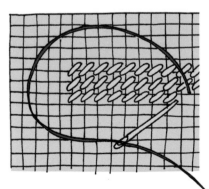

1 Start by practicing on a scrap of fabric to learn the stitch. Following the stitch diagram and working from left to right, bring your needle up from the back to the front at 1, then take the needle and go back through the fabric to the back at 2. Repeat this stitch by coming up at 3 and going back down at 4. Repeat this for the next two stitches. Work the next row in that color by working right to left, coming up at 9 and going down at 10 (so you are working the stitch from bottom left to top right). Repeat these stitches along the row.

2 Trace out the design from the template on page 125 and transfer onto the Aida fabric (see page 8). Stitch the design. Leave 1 in. (2.5 cm) at the top and left side of the fabric. Start at the top of the design, working from left to right, and stitch the first area of the design. To finish off and to start a new area of color, work the thread through a few stitches on the reverse to secure the ends and then snip off.

3 When you have completed all of the design, you may find that the cloth has become a bit distorted. If so then you will need to block the fabric, to restore it to its true shape. Spray the piece with some warm water—without saturating it too much—to relax the fibers. Pull it back into shape and pin it to a wooden board using the mapping pins. Leave this to dry—this could take a couple of days. You can repeat this process if it is still a bit distorted. Your piece is now ready to frame.

COPPER HOOP MACRAMÉ

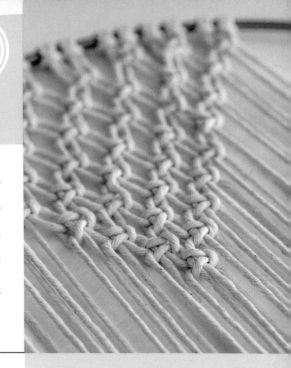

It's easy to see why macramé has come back into favor in recent years. It's fun and **RELAXING** to do, and once you've learnt the knots you can make beautiful and contemporary wall hangings. As your **MIND ENGAGES** with making the knots, it will help you to leave your worries behind and **DESTRESS.** This simple but effective piece, worked on a copper ring, is great if you're new to macramé.

1 Take one length of string, fold it in half and hold the loop in front of the hoop at the top. Fold the loop over the back of the hoop and thread the ends of the string through this loop to secure it to the hoop. Attach all the lengths of string, next to each other, in this way.

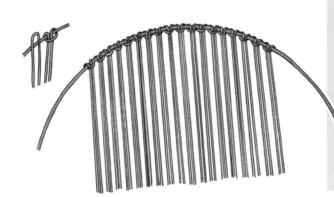

YOU WILL NEED

18 lengths of string, each measuring about 60 in. (1.5 m)

Copper or metal ring, 10 in. (25 cm) in diameter

Scissors

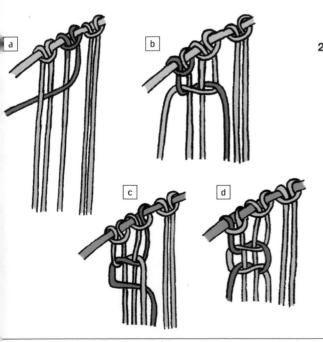

2 Start by working on the first four strands. Follow the diagram to form a square knot: take the right-hand strand and position it over the two center strands and under the right-hand strand (a). Move the left-hand strand behind the two center strands and pass it through the loop from behind (b). Repeat the above, this time starting with the strand on the left (c and d). Tighten the knot by pulling the two outer strands gently while holding the two center cords straight. Try and keep the knot flat and even and close to the rim of the hoop.

3 Repeat step 2 on the next four strands to make another square knot. At first it seems complicated and you have to study the step diagram every time but when you have completed a few it gets easier!

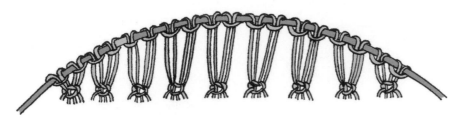

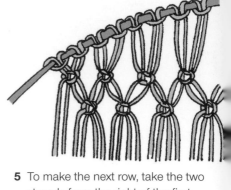

4 Continue making square knots on each group of four strands of string. Try and get the knots in a straight line, so that each knot as it gets to the middle of the row is made slightly further away from the hoop, and then on the second half of the row they move closer to it. You will end up with nine knots.

5 To make the next row, take the two strands from the right of the first square knot you made and the two strands from the left of the second knot you made. Use these four strands to make a square knot below and in between the two knots above. Repeat, taking the two free strands from the second square knot and two strands from the third square knot. Continue along the row, trying to keep the knots in a straight line as before. You will end up with eight knots.

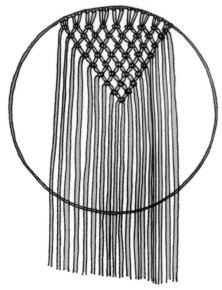

6 On the next row leave the first four strands and then repeat Step 5 to make seven knots; on the next row leave the first six strands free and complete six knots and on the next row leave the first eight strands free and complete five knots. Continue in this way, making one less knot each row, to form a triangle of knots, until you have just one knot in the middle.

7 Now you need to attach all the strings to the other side of the hoop. Taking two strands at a time, join them to the hoop as shown in the diagram and pull taut. Continue until all the stings are attached and are straight and taut.

8 Now make a second triangle of knots: leave the first four strands and then complete square knots across the row as before. There should be seven on the first row, then six, then five, finishing with one. Trim the ends of the strings in a straight line.

CORAL-INSPIRED EMBROIDERY HOOPS

Take your time and be **MINDFUL** as you work each stitch. **TUNE IN** to your breathing and purposely **SLOW YOUR PACE**. Embroidery hoops come in all sizes and are a lovely way of showing off and displaying your pieces. A group of different designs based around the same theme makes a charming and unusual piece of wall art. These designs, inspired by coral and sea plants, would fit perfectly into both a contemporary or traditional interior.

YOU WILL NEED

Three pieces of fabric–I used a mix of thin cottons and silk

Scissors

Stitch designs on pages 118–119

Tracing paper

Masking tape

Sharp pencil

Six-stranded embroidery floss (thread)

Embroidery and sewing needles

3 embroidery hoops: 4 in. (10 cm), 4¾ in. (12 cm), and 7 in. (18 cm) in diameter

1 Cut out three pieces of fabric to the following sizes: 6¾ x 6¾ in. (17 x 17 cm), 7½ x 7½ in. (19 x 19 cm), 10 x 10 in. (25 x 25 cm).

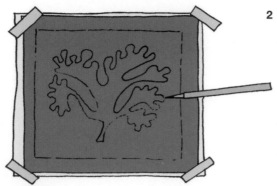

2 Trace out the designs on pages 118–119 and transfer them onto the fabric pieces. The designs are drawn showing the edge of the hoop to help you get the positioning right. Position the template so that there is a 1¼ in. (3.5 cm) border of fabric all around. For lighter fabrics I use a lightbox, but taping the template to a window and placing the fabric over the top works well too. Use a sharp pencil to draw onto the fabric, so that the lines are fine enough to be covered by the stitching.

3 If you are using a dark fabric for the smaller designs, you may not be able to see through it to trace the design. In that case, cut out the main shape from your tracing paper and place it in position on the fabric. Draw around it with a fine black pen—when you come to the embroidery, the stitching will cover the lines. I tend to just draw a few guidelines by hand and then stitch each line following the previously stitched line. (You could also use transfer paper—see the Techniques section on page 8.)

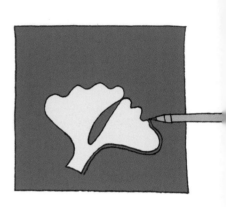

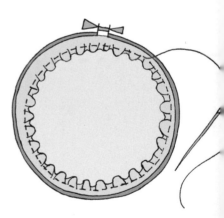

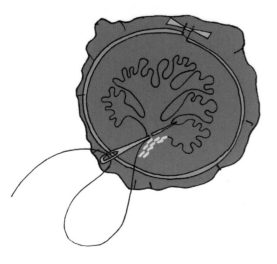

4 Secure the fabric into its corresponding hoop and start stitching the design. The design on the smallest hoop is whipped backstitch using a single strand of embroidery floss (thread), as I wanted the stitching to be delicate. The other two designs both use two strands of embroidery floss. The medium-sized design on the orange fabric is made by stitching bullion knots close together and the larger design is created using straight stitch (see on pages 10–11 for more on stitches and how to do them).

5 When you have finished stitching the design, thread any loose ends at the back through the stitching and trim back the fabric border to about ¾ in. (2 cm) all round. With a needle and thread make a line of running stitch all around, about ¼ in. (5 mm) in from the edge. Pull the thread to gather up the fabric and pull it in tight. Finish off the thread with a knot to secure.

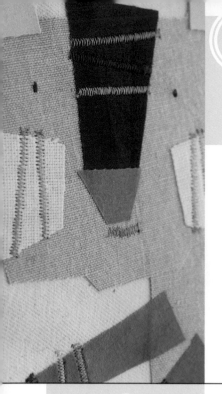

LEAPING TIGER WALL ART

You can use small scraps of leftover fabric to create this **JOYFUL** artwork, which is so **EASY** to make. I've given you a template to follow as a guide, but really you can fill in the spaces exactly how you want, cutting out different stripes and deciding where the lines of stitching go. I used mostly a selection of plain fabrics, but why not bring some patterns into the mix? Really **ANYTHING GOES** with this kind of appliqué work—even florals! It is all about having fun.

YOU WILL NEED

Template on page 124

Paper and pencil

Scissors

Scraps of fabric in different colors

A sheet of fusible bonding web (such as Wonderweb), about 20 x 20 in. (50 x 50 cm)

Iron

Canvas or thick cotton, 19 x 13 in. (48 x 34 cm)

Two bulldogs clips to hang the wall art

1 Using the template on page 124, transfer the shapes for the head, body, and legs onto paper. Cut these out so that you can use them to draw around.

2 Take a piece of fabric that you want to use as the base for the head and body of the tiger. Follow the instructions on your fusible web to iron it onto the wrong side of the piece of fabric you have chosen. Don't remove the backing paper yet. Do the same for the fabric you are using for the legs.

3 Use the templates to draw around and cut out the head and body and legs.

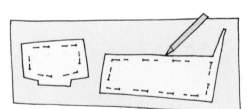

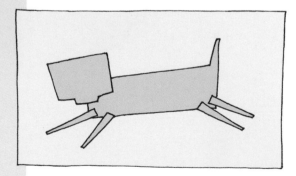

4 Lay them down in position on the canvas fabric, making sure that the tiger is centered on the canvas, with an even border all around. Once you are happy with the position, peel off the backing paper and follow the instructions on the fusible web to iron down and secure.

5 Iron some fusible bonding web onto the scraps of fabric you are using for the stripes and details on the face. Leave the whiskers for the moment. Cut out some shapes and start laying them down on the base tiger. You can keep moving them around until you are happy with the composition. I like the stripes to extend beyond the edges of the base shape as it makes a livelier image. When you are happy peel off the backing paper and iron these down.

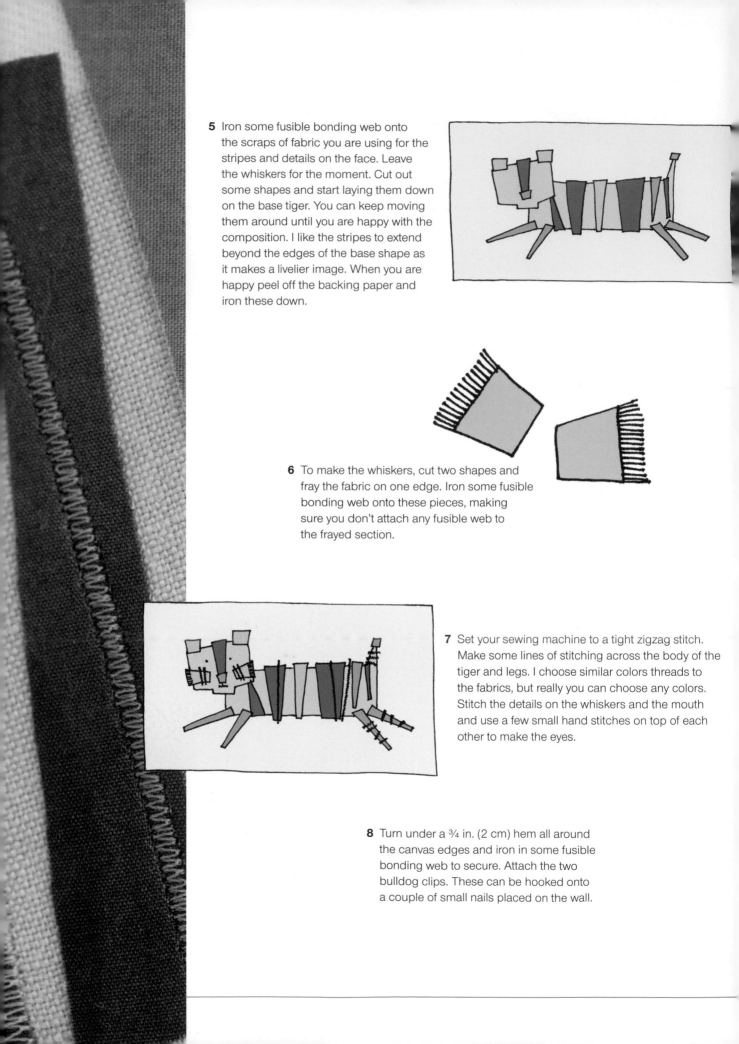

6 To make the whiskers, cut two shapes and fray the fabric on one edge. Iron some fusible bonding web onto these pieces, making sure you don't attach any fusible web to the frayed section.

7 Set your sewing machine to a tight zigzag stitch. Make some lines of stitching across the body of the tiger and legs. I choose similar colors threads to the fabrics, but really you can choose any colors. Stitch the details on the whiskers and the mouth and use a few small hand stitches on top of each other to make the eyes.

8 Turn under a ¾ in. (2 cm) hem all around the canvas edges and iron in some fusible bonding web to secure. Attach the two bulldog clips. These can be hooked onto a couple of small nails placed on the wall.

ART DECO WALL HANGING

I can't get enough of punch needling! I have one project set up on my frame to work on when I have a SPARE MINUTE, or when I want to UNWIND and RELAX but prefer to be doing something at the same time. The only drawback—if it really is a drawback—is that it is quite addictive and once you start, you want to keep going and fill in the next section. One thing for sure is that you will be SUPER-CHILLED after a session with your punch needle! I choose a monochrome palette, but this would also look wonderful worked in bright, vibrant colors.

YOU WILL NEED

Template on page 119

Paper, pencil, and pen

Sticky tape

Wooden frame (see page 9)—mine measured 10¾ x 16¾ in. (27 x 42 cm), which is big enough for this design, but you can use a larger frame and just cut the fabric down to size after completing the design

Monk's cloth or a loose weave linen fabric—enough to cover the frame with an extra 2½ in. (6 cm extra fabric around three of the sides and 6½ in. (16 cm) at the top (this is more than you need but is useful in case the fabric goes on the frame not exactly in position

Thick felt cut into 1½ in. (4 cm) strips

Needle and basting (tacking) thread

No. 10 punch needle

Chunky yarn in four different colors

Fine yarn for sewing the details

Small pointed scissors

Pins

Sewing machine

12 in. (30 cm) dowel, ¼ in. (5 mm) in diameter

1 Using the template on page 119, follow steps 1–6 of the Big and Bold Leaf Pillow on page 20 to transfer the design onto the cloth, attach it to the frame, and punch the design.

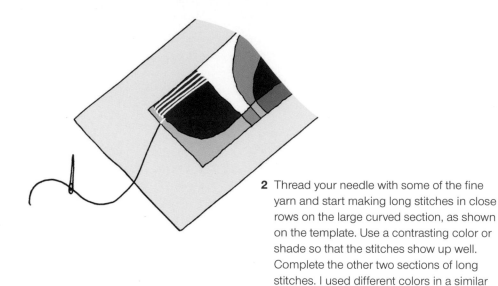

2 Thread your needle with some of the fine yarn and start making long stitches in close rows on the large curved section, as shown on the template. Use a contrasting color or shade so that the stitches show up well. Complete the other two sections of long stitches. I used different colors in a similar palette for these sections.

3 Trim the two long sides down so that the border measures 3½ in. (9 cm) up to the edge of the punched section. Do the same along the bottom edge. The top edge should be trimmed to 6¾ in. (17 cm).

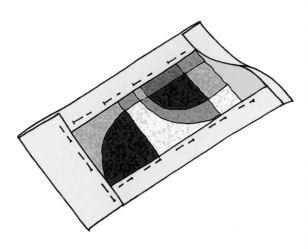

4 Turn over a ½ in. (1 cm) hem around all four edges, then fold over the fabric so that the fold of the hem aligns with the edge of the punched section. Pin in place. Hand stitch all around to secure—you can sew into the looped, punched section so the stitches won't show on the front.

TAKE A MOMENT...
The process of punch needling, and the feel of the yarns and natural linen mean this project is the very essence of mindful crafting, where the activity of making is as important as the result.

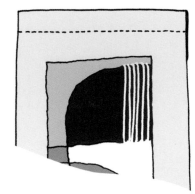

5 Sew a line of stitching across the width of the fabric 1¼ in. (3 cm) down from the top edge to make a channel. Push the length of dowel through to hang the wall art from.

DELICATE FLORAL WALL HANGING

I chose the palest pink for this delicate embroidered piece. The edges are raw and slightly frayed, and when hung from a small twig the finished work is elegant and makes a charming piece of art. There is a template for the stem, then the rest is up to you to fill in—sometimes it's good not to have a design to follow. It's a very **LIBERATING** and **CREATIVE** way to work because it means that once you're **IMMERSED** in the stitching, you don't have to stop to look at a pattern, making it a much more **RELAXING** experience!

YOU WILL NEED

Template on page 120

Tracing paper and pencil

Sticky tape (optional)

Piece of fabric, 8 x 11 in.
(20 x 28 cm)

Six-stranded embroidery
floss (thread)

Needle

Twig

TAKE A MOMENT...
Making a wall hanging is a gentle way to remind yourself to stay mindful once you've finished crafting. As it hangs on your wall, it will bring calm to your space.

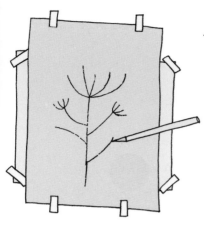

1 Using the template on page 120 and some tracing paper, transfer the design onto the fabric, choosing your preferred method (the different methods for transferring onto fabric are explained on page 8). Make sure the design is centered and starts about 1½ in. (4 cm) from the bottom edge. Because the fabric I used is quite pale, I was able to trace the template using a window as a lightbox.

2 Thread your needle with two strands of embroidery floss (thread). Stitch the stem, using whipped backstitch (see page 10).

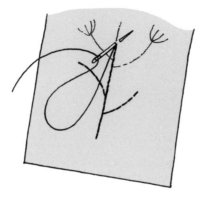

3 Starting at the top of one section of stem, start making the little flower shapes in daisy stitch (see page 10). I used one strand of embroidery floss (thread), as I wanted the stitching to be really delicate. Use the photograph as a guide to roughly follow the areas I filled in. Make the flowers in different sizes and group them together, so the petals touch each other.

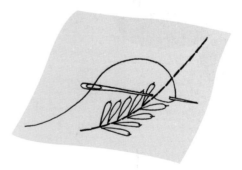

4 Stitch the leaves on either side of each leaf stem using detached chain stitch (see page 10).

5 Fray the edges of the fabric by pulling out some of the threads, then take a few of these threads and group them together. Thread a needle with the strands and make two loops at the top of the panel by bring the needle through from the back about 1¼ in. (3 cm) in from the side edge and ½ in. (1 cm) down from the top edge. Take the needle over the top to the back to create a loop and secure with a couple of small stitches.

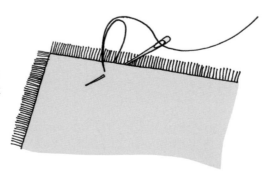

6 Place the twig in the loops ready for hanging.

TEXTURED WEAVE

YOU WILL NEED

A simple loom

Cotton knitting yarn or li[n]
thread for the warp thre[ad]

A large darning needl[e]

Yarn (a selection of bulk[y]
chunky and super bulk[y]
super chunky)

Scissors

A hoop for hanging

Masking tape

Sewing thread

In recent years there has been a revival in popularity of many crafts—weaving is one of them and it's easy to see why. You can create beautiful and original pieces that look stunning as wall hangings, and it is not hard to learn the basics. It is nice to vary the thickness of your yarn, but if you are making a weave all from triangles, like I have done here, it's is best to stick to two weights of yarn, bulky (chunky) and super bulky (super chunky). If you are new to weaving you may like to start by doing some freeform weaving, where you get started and design the weave as you go, EXPERIMENTING with different thicknesses and changing colors when you feel it is right. It can be a lovely LIBERATING WAY TO WORK, freeing your mind so that you can just CONCENTRATE on the ACTION of weaving. I have given instructions for this triangular design, but you may want to adapt it a bit, as your loom may be a different size and your yarn a different thickness. But that is the fun of it, you can even make up a triangle design as you go along!

NOTE

You can easily buy a basic loom from a craft store. You can also make a simple loom with a wooden frame and some small nails. Mark out across the top and bottom of the frame at ½ in. (1 cm) intervals. You need an even number of nails at each end. If you like the idea of making smaller triangle and diamond designs and intend to use fine yarn, then make the gaps smaller, about ¼ in. (5 mm). Use a small hammer to tap in the nails leaving about ½ in. (1 cm) raised.

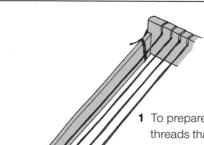

1 To prepare the loom with the warp threads (the threads that are held in tension along the loom) you can use yarn, but I prefer to use a cotton knitting yarn or thick linen thread. I find the tension is held well and there is less of a stretch. Tie one end of your thread around the side of the frame at the top. Wind the thread around a few times first, as this will give you some thread to tie off later. Slip it into the first notch or over the first nail and then take it along to the opposite notch or nail. Go into this notch or around the nail and along to the next notch or nail. Go into or around this one, and then back up to the top of the frame to the opposite notch or nail to this one. Keep doing this all along the loom. Tie off the thread at the end, to the side of the frame, making sure the tension is tight.

2 Now the fun starts! Cut a length of yarn and thread a darning needle. You can start from either side. Place the needle under the first strand and over the next and carry along the width, weaving under and over. Leave some yarn at the edge for tying off later.

3 Go back the other way, starting with an under, so that you are taking the yarn around the last strand and weaving back along the width again. When you reach the second to last warp, turn. Continue weaving turning one less strand on each row, making sure that you don't pull too tightly at the edges as this will make your weaving curve inward. If you need to add another length of yarn to your needle do this at the edge, taking the yarn under the warp and leaving a bit of yarn to tie off. When the triangle is complete take the yarn to the back of the weaving, leaving a bit of yarn to tie off.

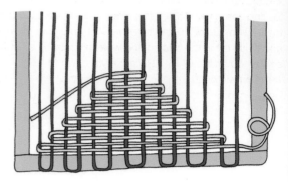

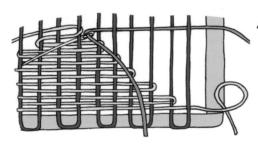

4 Thread up a needle with a different color. Start at the edge level with the top of the triangle you have already created and go under and over the warp as before. When you reach the point of the triangle, take the yarn under the warp in between the woven yarn and then go back out and return back along the row.

5 Continue in this way, going either under or over the warp in between the threads at the edge of the first triangle and then returning, until you have filled this area. You may have to practice this a few times. It is worth persevering and will soon seem so simple. Once you have mastered this, you can make all sorts of designs with triangles, chevrons, and diamonds. If your yarn is not thick enough to fill the space, you can double it up. Keep pushing the rows down, so that the weave looks even. You can do this with your fingers or, if you have bought a loom, it may have come with a wide wooden comb (a fork also works).

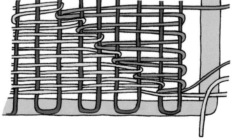

6 Repeat steps 4 and 5 on the other side of the first triangle. Then repeat these three triangles in reverse to make the next section of the design. Finally, repeat the first three triangles to make the top section of the design.

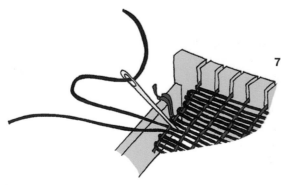

7 Next you need to tie off any bits of loose yarn. Any yarn that ended over the warp, take it around to the back of the weaving and push the needle under the weaving but not going through to the front. Bring the needle up away from the edge and secure with a knot. With the yarn strand that came under the warp, you need to thread that and push it down over the warp.

8 When you have finished, cut the warp ends at the bottom, leaving some yarn to tie off. Unloop the top end and cut the tied-on piece. Thread this spare bit onto your needle and finish off at the back of the weaving, leaving a similar sized loop as the others. Because you have used thick yarn you will need to ease the weaving up to fill the loops. Do the same at the bottom of the weaving, but leave the loops, don't pull the yarn down to cover them.

9 To add some tassels, cut some lengths of yarn about 12 in. (30 cm) in length. Take a few and group them together. Fold them in half and thread the loop through one of the loops at the bottom of the weaving. Take the strands of yarn back through the loop and pull gently to tighten. Continue all along the bottom and then trim to neaten. Adjust the bottom of the weaving so that any loop is covered up by easing the wool down slightly.

10 To make the hanging section you need some sort of hoop. Mine was part of a large key ring, but a large curtain hook wound work well. Cut 12 lengths of cotton yarn to about 18 in. (45 cm) and fold them in half. Take one loop to the back of the hoop, bring the ends up through the loop and pull to secure over the hoop. Repeat with the other 11 strands.

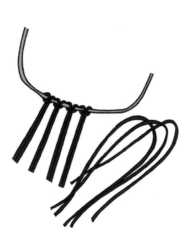

11 Lay the weaving face down. Spread the ends of the 12 strands evenly across the top of the weaving—the ones in the center will be a little shorter than the ones at the side—and secure the strands with a piece of masking tape. Make sure the weaving hangs straight and, if not, make a few adjustments. Use some sewing thread to stitch back and forth over each pair of yarn ends to secure, making sure that you do not take the thread through to the front. Remove the masking tape.

TEMPLATES

Most of the projects in this book use some kind of template, to be used either as a cutting or stitch guide. If a template needs to be enlarged it will clearly say by what percentage. See page 8 for more tips for using templates.

BIG AND BOLD LEAF PILLOW
page 20

50% of actual size, enlarge by 200%

SQUEEZY KITTY

page 90

50% of actual size,
enlarge by 200%

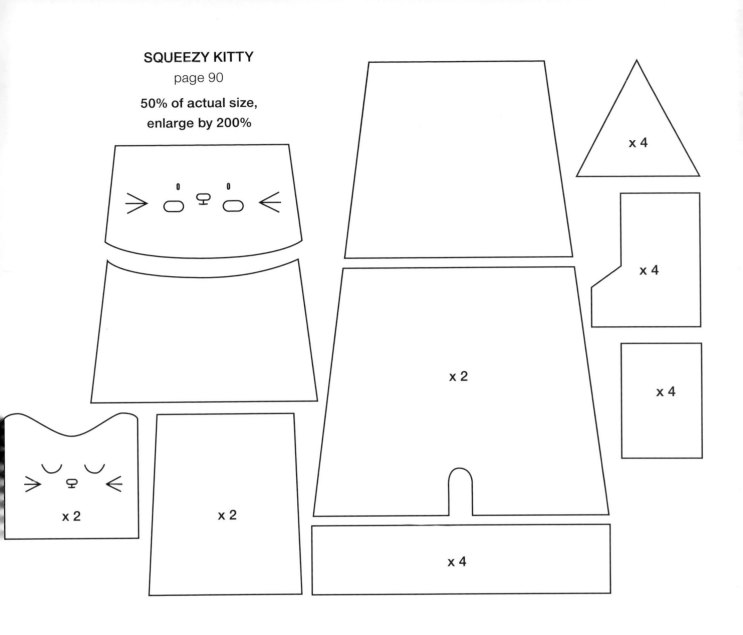

SCALLOP EDGED BABY QUILT

page 75

actual size

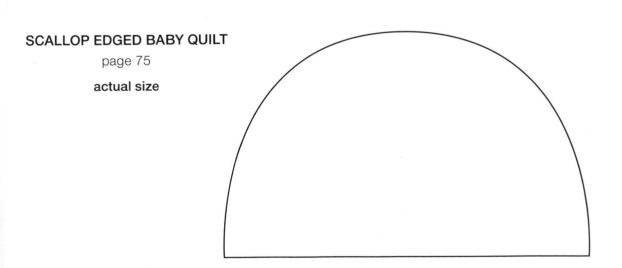

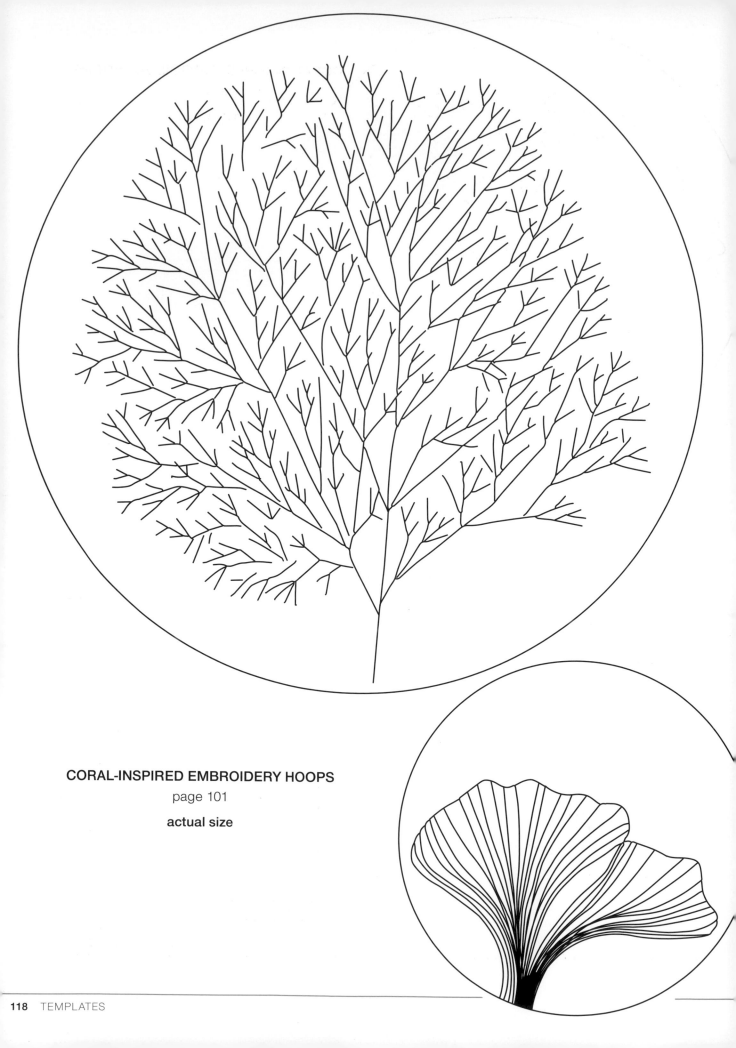

CORAL-INSPIRED EMBROIDERY HOOPS

page 101

actual size

CORAL-INSPIRED EMBROIDERY HOOPS

page 101

actual size

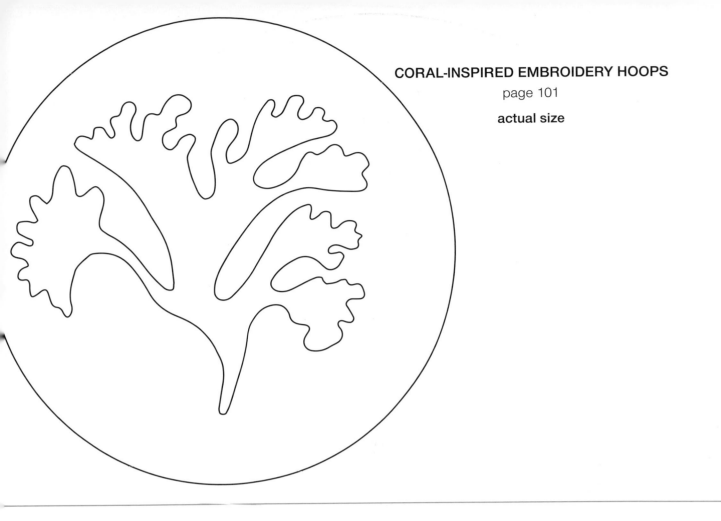

ART DECO WALL HANGING

page 107

50% of actual size, enlarge by 200%

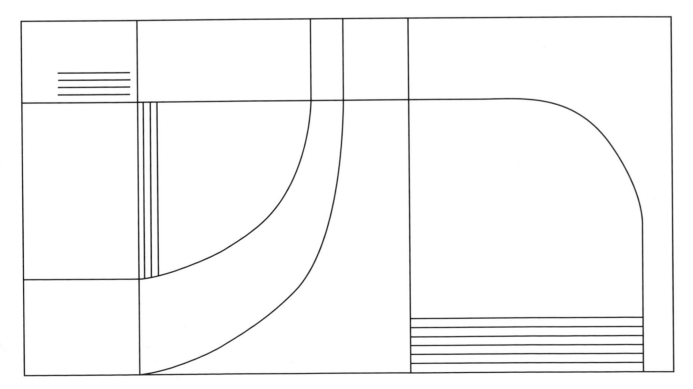

FLORAL NEEDLEPOINT CARDS
page 68
actual size

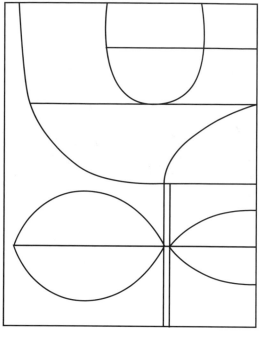

DELICATE FLORAL WALL HANGING
page 110
actual size

LITTLE ACORN COVERED BUTTONS
page 44
actual size

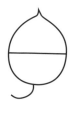

■ Whipped backstitch
■ Straight stitch
■ Bullion knot

KNOT STITCHED LINEN BAG
page 57

actual size

EMBROIDERED SHIRT
page 42

actual size

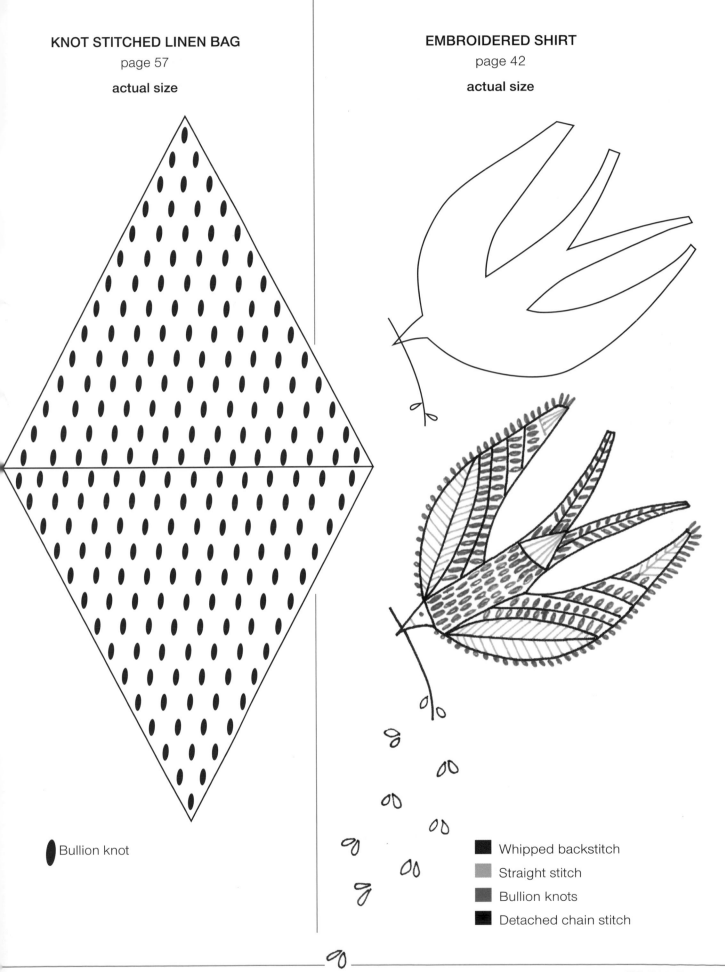

⬬ Bullion knot

⬛ Whipped backstitch

⬛ Straight stitch

⬛ Bullion knots

⬛ Detached chain stitch

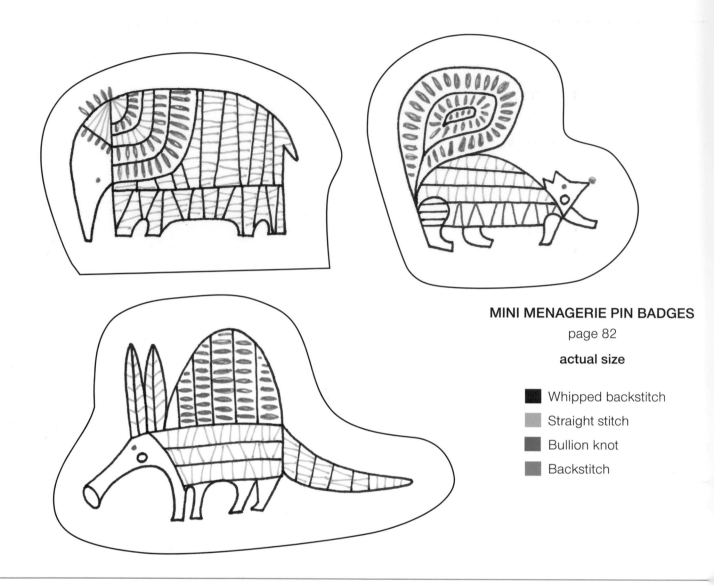

MINI MENAGERIE PIN BADGES

page 82

actual size

■	Whipped backstitch
■	Straight stitch
■	Bullion knot
■	Backstitch

SASHIKO STITCHED COASTERS

page 38

50% of actual size, enlarge by 200%

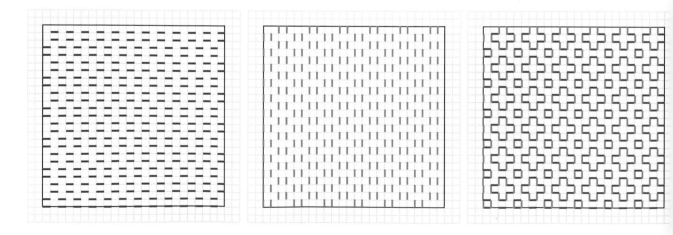

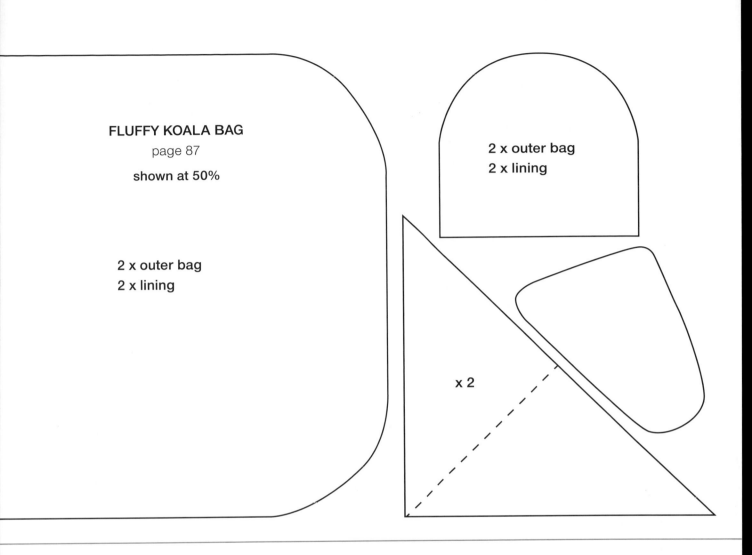

FLUFFY KOALA BAG
page 87

shown at 50%

2 x outer bag
2 x lining

2 x outer bag
2 x lining

x 2

LATCH HOOK PILLOW
page 26

50% of actual size,
enlarge by 200%

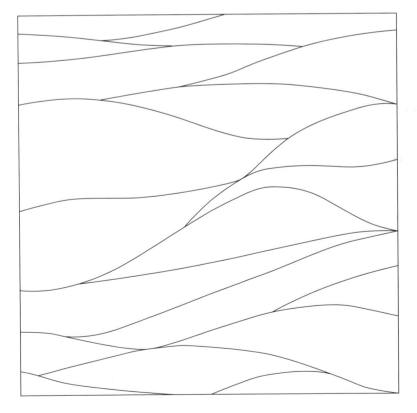

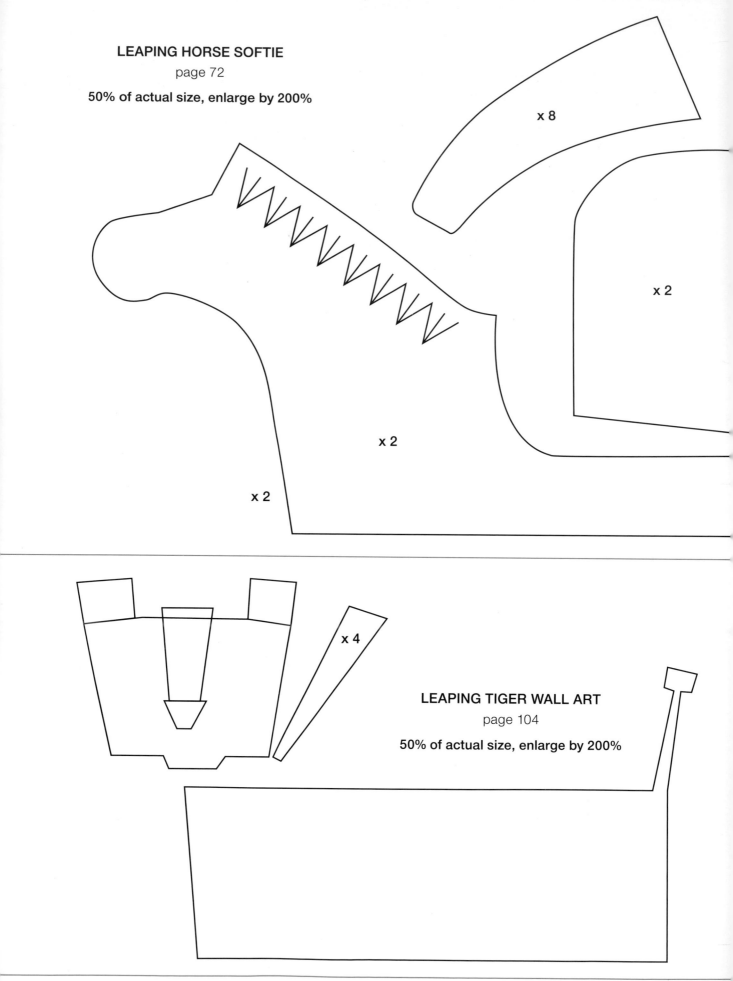

LEAPING HORSE SOFTIE

page 72

50% of actual size, enlarge by 200%

x 8

x 2

x 2

x 2

x 4

LEAPING TIGER WALL ART

page 104

50% of actual size, enlarge by 200%

RAINDROP CLOUD MOBILE

page 84

**50% of actual size,
enlarge by 200%**

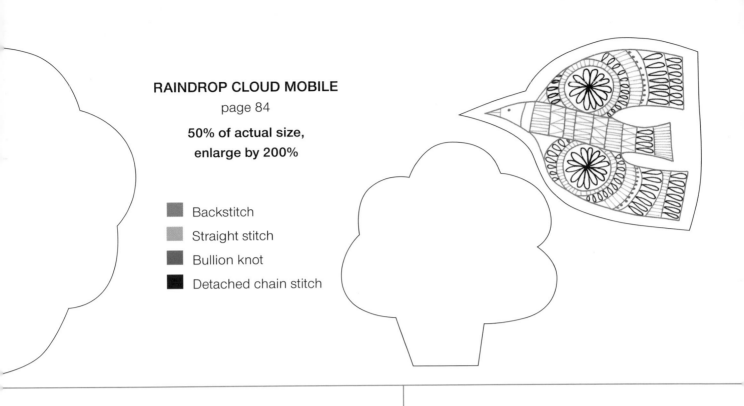

- Backstitch
- Straight stitch
- Bullion knot
- Detached chain stitch

PUNCH-NEEDLED FOOTSTOOL

page 18

25% of actual size, enlarge by 400%

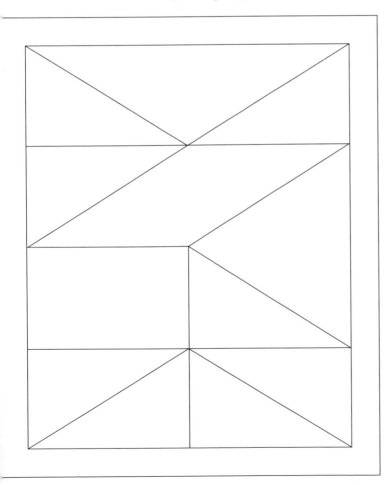

ABSTRACT FRAMED NEEDLEPOINT

page 96

50% of actual size, enlarge by 200%

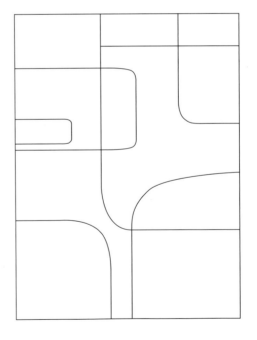

NORDIC CHRISTMAS STOCKINGS

page 78

25% of actual size, enlarge by 400%

x 2

x 2

SUPPLIERS

UK STOCKISTS

The Cloth House
020 7437 5155
www.clothhouse.com

C Wool
01843 862848
www.cwool.co.uk

Hobby Craft
0330 026 1400
www.hobbycraft.co.uk

John Lewis
03456 049 049
www.johnlewis.com

Liberty
020 7734 1234
www.libertylondon.com

London Loop (punch
needling supplies)
www.loopknittingshop.com

MacCulloch and Wallis
020 7629 0311
www.macculloch-wallis.co.uk

Ian Mankin
020 7722 0997
www.ianmankin.co.uk

Merchant & Mills
01797 227789
www.merchantandmills.com

V V Rouleaux
020 7224 5179
www.vvrouleaux.com

US STOCKISTS

Amy Butler
www.amybutlerdesign.com

Britex Fabrics
415-392-2910
www.britexfabrics.com

Discount Fabrics USA
301-271-2266
discountfabricsusacorp.com

Fabricland/Fabricville
www.fabricland.com
www. fabricland.ca

J & O Fabrics
856-663-2121
www.jandofabrics.com

Jo-Ann Fabric and Craft Store
330-735-6576
www.joann.com

Michaels
800-642-4235
www.michaels.com

The Oxford Company (punch
needling supplies)
802-462-2011
www.amyoxford.com

Purl Soho
800-597-7875
www.purlsoho.com

Tinsel Trading Company
510-570-2149
www.tinseltrading.com

Vogue Fabrics
800-433-4313
www.voguefabricsstore.com

Wazoodle
215-244-2504
www.wazoodle.com

INDEX

abstract framed needlepoint 96–7, 125

acorn covered buttons 44–5, 120

Art Deco wall art 107–9, 119

backstitch, whipped 10

badges, mini menagerie pin 82–3, 122

bags: fluffy koala bag 87–9, 123

knot stitched linen bag 57–9, 121

rainbow handled string bag 65–7

splatter tote bag 48–50

wave stitched craft bag 62–4

big and bold leaf pillow 20–2, 116

blanket stitch 10

boro stitched jeans 54–6

bowls, zigzag 29–31

bullion knot 11

buttons, little acorn covered 44–5, 120

cards, floral needlepoint 68–9, 120

chain stitch, detached 10

children, gifts for 70–93

Christmas stockings, Nordic 78–81, 126

coasters, sashiko stitched 38–9, 122

color block quilt 35–7

copper hoop macramé 98–100

coral-inspired embroidery hoops 101–3, 118–19

daisy stitch 10

decorations, tasseled tree 46–7

detached chain stitch 10

doodle notebooks 51–3

embroidery: coral-inspired embroidery hoops 101–3, 118–19

embroidered shirt 42–3, 121

sashiko stitched coaster 38–9, 122

felt planters 14–15

floral: delicate floral wall hanging 110–11, 120

floral needlepoint cards 68–9, 120

fluffy koala bag 87–9, 123

footstool, punch-needled 18–19, 125

French knot 11

horse softie, leaping 72–4, 124

indigo woven mat 23–5

jeans, boro stitched 54–6

jute-covered lamp 32–4

kitty, squeezy 90–3, 117

knot stitched linen bag 57–9, 121

koala bag, fluffy 87–9, 123

lamp, jute-covered 32–4

latch hook pillow 26–8, 123

leaping horse softie 72–4, 124

leaping tiger wall art 104–6, 124

leather pouches 60–1

macramé, copper hoop 98–100

mats, indigo woven 23–5

menagerie pin badges 82–3, 122

mobile, rainbow cloud 84–6, 125

motifs, transferring 8

needlepoint: abstract framed needlepoint 96–7, 125

floral needlepoint cards 68–9, 120

Nordic Christmas stockings 78–81, 126

notebooks, doodle 51–3

patterns, transferring 8

pillows: big and bold leaf pillow 20–2, 116

latch hook pillow 26–8, 123

planters, felt 14–15

pompom throw 16–17

pouches, soft leather 60–1

punch needling 9

big and bold leaf pillow 20–2, 116

punch-needled footstool 18–19, 125

quilts: color block quilt 35–7

scallop edged baby quilt 75–7, 117

rainbows: rainbow cloud mobile 84–6, 125

rainbow handled string bag 65–7

sashiko stitched coaster 38–9, 122

satin stitch 10

scallop edged baby quilt 75–7, 117

shirt, embroidered 42–3, 121

softie, leaping horse 72–4, 124

splatter tote bag 48–50

squeezy kitty 90–3, 117

stitches 10–11

stockings, Nordic Christmas 78–81, 126

straight stitch 10

tasseled tree decorations 46–7

techniques 8–11

templates 116–26

textured weave 112–15

throw, pompom 16–17

tiger wall art, leaping 104–6, 124

tote bag, splatter 48–50

tree decorations, tasseled 46–7

wall art 94–115

wave stitched craft bag 62–4

weave, textured 112–15

whipped backstitch 10

zigzag bowls 29–31

ACKNOWLEDGMENTS

I would like to thank everyone at CICO who made it possible for me to write a book on a subject dear to my heart. It is always a pleasure to work with the team who make everything come together so smoothly, especially Cindy, Anna, Sally, Penny, and Gurjant. Thank you to Jo Henderson for the beautiful and inspiring photography. Thanks to Clare Sayer for the careful editing and to Elizabeth Healey for the lovely design. Thank you to Ian for having the patience and skill to turn my roughs into the wonderful finished artworks. As always, a huge thanks to Milly, Florence, Henrietta, and Harvey, for their support, encouragement, and valuable advice.